AFRICAN ADVENTURE

◈

F. C. SELOUS

AFRICAN ADVENTURE

Letters from Famous Big-Game Hunters

Denis D. Lyell

◆

Peter Capstick, Series Editor

St. Martin's Press
New York

To the Reader:

The editors and publishers of the Peter Capstick Adventure Library faced significant responsibilities in the faithful reprinting of Africa's great hunting books of long ago. Essentially, they saw the need for each text to reflect to the letter the original work, nothing having been added or expunged, if it was to give the reader an authentic view of another age and another world.

In deciding that historical veracity and honesty were the first considerations, they realized that it meant retaining many distasteful racial and ethnic terms to be found in these old classics. The firm of St. Martin's Press, Inc., therefore wishes to make it very clear that it disassociates itself and its employees from the abhorrent racial-ethnic attitudes of the past which may be found in these books.

History is the often unpleasant record of the way things actually were, not the way they should have been. Despite the fact that we have no sympathy with the prejudices of decades past, we feel it better—and indeed, our collective responsibility—not to change the unfortunate facts that were.

—Peter Hathaway Capstick

AFRICAN ADVENTURE. Copyright © 1988 by Peter Hathaway Capstick. All rights reserved. Printed in the United States of America. No part of this book may be used or reproduced in any manner whatsoever without written permission except in the case of brief quotations embodied in critical articles or reviews. For information, address St. Martin's Press, 175 Fifth Avenue, New York, N.Y. 10010.

Library of Congress Cataloging-in-Publication Data

Lyell, Denis D.
  African adventure.

  "From Peter Capstick's library."
  1. Big game hunting—Africa. I. Title.
SK251.L817   1988   799.2'6'096   88-11471
ISBN 0-312-02149-6

First Edition

10 9 8 7 6 5 4 3 2 1

EDITOR'S NOTE TO THE REPRINT EDITION

Denis D. Lyell, the noted big game hunter and writer whose eight books on African hunting span three decades of bush adventures and have become highly prized collector's items, was a prince of a man whose friendship was valued by all his hunting peers. This book tells you why.

African Adventure is possibly Lyell's most unusual book in that it does not follow the general narrative form. Published in 1935, this book is now rare in its only edition, appearing as it did in the Depression years when there were virtually no large first printings, let alone second runs, on such specialized fare as African hunting. Destined to be Lyell's last book, it is a unique collection of letters he received from the great hunters of his time, the golden days of African hunting between the 1890s and the 1930s.

Lyell, whose *Memories of an African Hunter* features in this series, was born in Calcutta in 1871 and died in Scotland in 1946. He spent years in British Central Africa, now Malawi, and also hunted extensively in the adjoining Rhodesias and Portuguese East Africa. His integrity as a hunter and human being marked him early on as one of the few gentlemen hunters of Africa who became the confidant of men such as Selous, Bell, Stigand, Millais, J. A. Hunter, Sir Alfred Pease, Chapman, and many, many others. Their letters to him over the years give rare insight into their lives and accomplishments as they speak of hunters and hunting, reflecting a style quite different from what we usually see, for these hunters are writing private thoughts to an esteemed friend, a man who became the doyen of the hunting fraternity, a man without malice who never backstabbed his fellow hunters and who was always prepared to listen.

As a collection of private documents, *African Adventure* has no equal in published African hunting literature. As such, it is essential to any library of hunting Africana, however casual. Of course, the strength of the book rests not only on the fine reputation of Lyell himself but on the reputations of the contributors, many of whom were dead by the time this book saw light. Frederick Courteney Selous had been killed by a German bullet, fighting as a sixty-five-year-old captain in the 25th Royal Fusiliers, the "Legion of Frontiersmen" at Beho-Beho in East Africa on 4 January 1917. Gone too were Millais, Selous's biographer, R. J. Cunninghame, Teddy Roosevelt's professional hunter in 1919, Stigand—speared to death in 1919 by the Aliab Dinka—Ryan, and Chapman. Their letters, then, are their own eulogy to a time and place we can never know in the same way but which we can savor through the talent and foresight of Lyell himself.

African Adventure can be thought of as a thick packet of mail from some twenty of the best-known African hunters of the day. The letters vary from short notes to quite lengthy writings, expertly annotated by Lyell into a collection of intimate profiles that are never seen by the public through the books written by many of the contributors. Some of the letters are bright with joy of recent trips to places which no longer have the same names. Others are truly depressing.

By way of example: Imagine the hopelessness of an ageing Sir Alfred Pease, celebrated hunter, author, and pioneer whose *The Book of the Lion* features in this reprint series. His life had altered to such an extent that he mentioned to Lyell that he could no longer afford to buy books on his beloved

Africa but merely read reviews of them in the newspapers. What could have gone wrong? Poor, poor old boy.

And Selous, the incomparable hunter-naturalist and author. Talked into writing *African Nature Notes and Reminiscenses* by Theodore Roosevelt, he tells Lyell that there is no money at all in writing books and that an author is far better off to stick with magazine articles! Stigand announced to Lyell his intention of producing a "bread-winning book," an obvious reference to *Hunting the Elephant in Africa,* which is also featured in this series and which was to become prized Africana. R. J. Cunninghame gives his reasons for never having attempted to write of his often amazing African experiences. And anyone who has gone through the trials of a first book can only agree with his pseudo-comical justification. All the more reason why Lyell's fine prose and solid information are now so valuable; he rescued the names and feats of the better hunters from eventual oblivion, adding their names to our African hunting heritage.

I find the most interesting aspect of *African Adventure* to be the free discussion of the real experts when writing to Lyell, their friend and equal, concerning different calibers, rifle types, the relative danger of different species of game, and the hundreds of intuitive bits of information that never appear in any formal book directed at a commercial audience. Where else would one be given a detailed description on how to make a slingshot? It was Millais who wrote to Lyell and advised that one should ". . . keep the rubber warm in trousers pocket for two days before using." This, from a big game hunter of renown! Here, then, is your chance to sit in on a discussion around a campfire long, long dead. There is the jealousy and the admiration, controversy and hardship, excitement and sadness as Lyell, always the impartial referee and trusted friend, guides you on hunts in many African countries. An era is recreated where foot safaris were the norm and it was by no means uncommon for mailbags to be eaten by lions.

The letters reveal the inherent dangers of African hunting. Selous, for example, tells of a miraculous escape by one of his companions from a lioness, while Stigand survived a goring by a black rhino, a mauling by a lion, and the invasion of his house by a leopard that was after his dog! How ironic that the elephant hunter T. Alexander Barns was to die under a train in Chicago after surviving a croc attack and many close shaves with jumbo.

A. L. Barnshaw, one of the early elephant hunters of British Central Africa, amply demonstrated the old maxim that "it's the dead ones that get up and kill you" when he wrote to Lyell of a near-fatal encounter with an elephant he was sure was dead. And Norman Smith, a remarkable man to whom this book is dedicated, once wrote to Lyell that buffalo was "the worst of dangerous game to stop once he starts."

This collection of letters is your ticket to adventure in many countries where life was precarious not only because of the dangers of hunting but because of diseases such as malaria, sleeping sickness, and dysentery. The hunters of those days were a tough breed and, had it not been for Lyell's writings, we would not have had nearly so complete a picture of them and the times in which they lived.

Lyell, a fair-chase advocate and the epitome of moderation, is a wonderful example for any hunter, particularly the young hunter, to emulate. He, like so many of us who followed later, fell prey to Africa's charms and retained that magic in his soul to the end. In thinking back on a par-

ticular night in camp near the Luangwa River, my old
hunting haunts, Lyell writes:

> Sitting by a camp fire in the African bush with natives
> and game trophies about always made me feel roman-
> tic, and the memory of that evening, simple as it was,
> recalls the glamour Africa used to throw on me, and
> its everlasting lure to those who love the wild and
> primitive.
>
> —PETER HATHAWAY CAPSTICK

CONTENTS

LIST OF ILLUSTRATIONS

PREFACE

THIS small volume contains some of the letters I have received during the last thirty years or more from well-known big-game hunters and field-naturalists, many of whom have now passed away.

They were so interesting to me that I thought they might interest others who have shot in wilder Africa. Moreover, they describe conditions which are no longer possible considering the way many parts of that continent have been opened up since the Great War.

Whether the spread of a so-called civilization is a good thing I do not wish to discuss, but I know there are many men, including myself, who would prefer the older times when things were less complicated and conventional.

Many people are now going in for photography more than shooting, and in a way this is a good thing as it will naturally help to conserve the game. It is, however, a much less risky amusement to take animals' pictures—I mean dangerous animals—than to try to kill them, for game such as lion, elephant, buffalo, leopard and rhinoceros are seldom dangerous until they are wounded and followed up in

thick cover. Some people may doubt this statement, but it is nevertheless true, as all experienced
hunters can vouch.

For their kind permission to use letters and other
writings, and in some cases photographs, my best
thanks are due to the following : Mrs. F. C. Selous,
Mrs. J. G. Millais, Lady Charles Kennedy (formerly
Mrs. R. J. Cuninghame), Mrs. Moore (formerly
Mrs. C. H. Stigand), Mrs. Charles Sheldon, Sir
Alfred E. Pease, Bt., Lt.-Col. J. Stevenson-Hamilton,
Brig.-Gen. Sir Robert Pigot, Bt., D.S.O., M.C.,
Major C. E. Radclyffe, Major W. D. M. Bell,
Capt. J. Brander-Dunbar, D.L., Mr. Norman B.
Smith, Mr. George Garden, Capt. T. Chapman,
Mr. H. S. P. Maitland and Mr. J. F. Brown.

There are a few others whose letters I give, such
as Mr. Leslie Tarlton and Mr. A. Blayney Percival,
whom I have not asked for permission to use letters,
but I am sure they will not mind as there is nothing
in them which can hurt anyone's feelings.

I have been unable to get into touch with Mrs.
Barns, the widow of my old friend, the late T.
Alexander Barns, whom I knew well in north-
eastern Rhodesia, and who long ago gave me the
photograph of himself with an elephant. Barns
was not only a fine elephant hunter, but an able
field-naturalist, collector and photographer.

With regard to the accounts of sport in this book,
many may think that some of the old hunters shot
too much, but it must be remembered that game
was much more plentiful then, and owing to the

fact that their equipment was nearly always carried by porters they had many natives to feed, and a healthy African savage is a hungry mortal. I have seen some of my men eat quite 10 lbs. of meat when sitting by a camp fire at night.

Again, the only way a white hunter could persuade the natives to act as carriers was the promise and prospect of plenty of red meat.

Many of the white hunters, the first of our race to break into new country, were such fine men that they gained for Britishers a prestige that still holds good. In older days in southern Africa Capt. William Cornwallis Harris, Roualeyn Gordon Cumming, William Cotton Oswell and William Charles Baldwin set a very high standard; and later this standard has been well maintained by the men whose letters appear herein. Where Selous, Stigand, Bell and Cuninghame have been, to mention only a few, there still exists amongst the natives a feeling of respect and trust, which it is to be hoped the present representatives of our race will uphold. Civilization, when rushed, has an unhappy way of spoiling the coloured races in our oversea possessions, and some of us who have known them in a primitive state prefer them so, for then they are natural and unspoilt, but as Mr. Kipling remarks: " This is another story! "

I would like to say a few words to the young sportsman who may find himself in a good game district in Africa. The game regulations will naturally limit the numbers of the various species he can shoot, but these, in some cases, are fixed on rather a generous scale. Let him go for the really good male heads, leaving alone all the inferior males and sparing all females.

A true sporting instinct and a full sense of fair play towards man or beast is largely inherited, and is often the result of a decent upbringing, but it can also be learnt from the example of those who have practised moderation and restraint. I have heard of some extremely unsporting actions in Africa. Probably some of these were caused by thoughtlessness, and the excitement which overcomes certain individuals when they find themselves loose in Africa armed with quick-firing modern weapons.

An expert hunter does not fire at game until he is well in range of his quarry. He carefully picks his spot, and often waits some time until the position of the animal is suitable. He concentrates all his attention on the single beast he has picked as being the best male trophy. He would never think of spraying bullets promiscuously at various members of a herd, for in such a nefarious proceeding not one bullet out of ten will strike a beast correctly. The result of such a disgraceful action simply means that many beautiful and innocent creatures are sent away grievously wounded, when they will be shunned by the other members of their kind, and be a helpless prey to the carnivora which feed on them.

A beginner often finds it very difficult to exercise control over his nervous system when he gets close to his intended victim, particularly when the animal may be classed as " dangerous." This used to be termed " buck fever," and there is no doubt this intense feeling of excitement often leads to extremely bad shooting, and consequently wounding instead of killing.

Whether slaying wild creatures is justifiable or not, I do not wish to discuss to any great length, although I believe there is quite as much justification for shooting animals with a sporting rifle as there is for killing them in an abattoir. Animals forced into the reeking blood fumes of a slaughter-house probably suffer much more than any creature shot in the open ; and, of course, it is pure nonsense for meat-eaters to decry the sportsman, who has every bit as much moral right to kill animals himself as those who have it done for them.

Finally, to the novice I would say that when it comes to the finish he will find it a supreme satisfaction to know that throughout his sporting career he has always practised a code of moderation and restraint.

To Lord Gorell, C.B.E., M.C., I wish to express my sincere thanks for the interest he has taken in this book.

DENIS D. LYELL.

Rossdhal,
   Comrie,
      Perthshire.
February, 1935.

CHAPTER I

Capt. F. C. Selous, D.S.O.

THE letters which follow are memories from the past, and they were mostly written by men who have now gone. Some of them are amongst our most noted big-game hunters and naturalists, and their names will live so long as Britons take an interest in adventure and the study of wild life in the out-of-the-way places of the earth. Nearly every one of these letters refers to African sport and natural history, and I begin this volume by quoting some of the more interesting of those I received from the late F. C. Selous, D.S.O., whose life was packed with adventure, and whose gallant death at the age of sixty-four was a fitting end to his remarkable career. Many men have shot more elephants and lions than Selous, but very few have been able to describe the life of an African hunter better than he did, or to give us such interesting notes on the life histories of the game he hunted.

Here is the first letter I received from him :

" (Alpine Lodge, Worplesdon, Surrey, 9/9/1898.)
" As you already have a fairly powerful rifle (the ·500 bore) I would certainly recommend you to get

one of the new small bore rifles (Lee-Metford, Mauser or Mannlicher) in preference either to a Martini-Henry or heavy 10 bore gun for ball.

"I killed ten elephants (six out of one herd), besides some rhinoceroses and many buffaloes, with a ·450 bore Metford express, using a long solid bullet, and therefore think you will find your ·500 bore express quite powerful enough for these animals, whilst for all the large African antelopes one of the new small bore rifles is undoubtedly the best weapon.

"Since 1895 I have been using a ·303 by Holland. I shot with it about 50 animals in Africa, and found that it killed Sable and Roan antelopes, Koodoos, etc., very satisfactorily. Last year I also killed with it in America 7 Wapiti bulls—all that I fired at with it. I have always used Holland's ' peg ' bullets, which expand very well on large and small animals. I have never shot a lion with a ·303 rifle, but would not hesitate to do so if I got the chance, as I feel sure that a ' peg ' bullet from one of these small bore rifles would kill a lion very easily.

"My friend Mr. R. T. Coryndon, who shot a lot in South Africa, and is now stationed in the Barotze Valley, on the Upper Zambezi, uses nothing but a ·303 by Holland. He kills buffaloes with the solid bullets. With your double ·500 and a ·303 I think you will be all right with every kind of African game.

"For elephants in dense jungle, where you cannot

pick your shots, a very heavy rifle or smooth bore might be better than any other weapon, but unless you intend to devote yourself exclusively to elephant hunting I would not burden myself with such a weapon and heavy ammunition.

" I believe you will like a ·303 rifle with 'peg' bullets very much, but I am not at all sure that the Mannlicher is not the best of all the small bore rifles. Littledale and Sir E. Loder use nothing else, and· Mr. E. N. Buxton used one in Somaliland and was well pleased with it. However, the difference between the relative merits of the ·303, the Mauser and the Mannlicher rifles is not very great. They are all wonderful weapons, and in my opinion you ought to have one of them with you in East Africa, and with that and your ·500 you will find yourself all right.

" Wishing you the best of luck.

(Signed) " F. C. SELOUS."

"PS.—Some day, at some odd moment, perhaps you will be able to send me a line letting me know how you get on in East Africa. I should like very much to hear from you."

This was the first letter I got from Selous in answer to seeking his advice about the modern ·303 and other bores. After that we exchanged many letters. The next letter is from " Heatherside," and Selous had evidently changed the name of his house in Surrey, or changed his residence.

" (Heatherside, Worplesdon, Surrey, 13/1/1904.)

" I was very much interested in your letter of Nov. 20th, which reached me a few days ago.

" You seem to be having a very pleasant time in B.C.A. [British Central Africa or Nyasaland] and I hope that you will soon get a good billet in the Administration.

" This time last year I was in East Africa along the Uganda Railway. There is a great deal of game in that country, and I added a good many new specimens to my collection, but my trip was very much spoiled by incessant rain, and the consequent long wet grass. The season was, however, quite an unusually wet one, and I hope to have better luck this year as I intend going to East Africa again about July, as from all I can learn August, September and October are usually dry months. I made a little trip to Sardinia last October, after Moufflon, but there again I was very much hindered by heavy rain, and consequent dense mists, which made all hunting impossible as long as they lasted. I got six Moufflon, however, four pretty good ones amongst them. I have not written anything lately. The last thing I wrote was an account of a trip I made, in 1900 I think, to Newfoundland after Caribou. This was published in three numbers of the *Wide World Magazine*. If you have not seen them I will send them to you.

" By the bye, can Koodoos and Buffaloes still be got in B.C.A. ? People often ask me where they can go to get heads of these animals.

" Now goodbye, and wishing you the very best of luck, and hoping you will come and see me on your return to this country.

(Signed) " F. C. SELOUS."

Then, omitting several other letters, I come to one written when Selous was staying with Sir Philip Brocklehurst, where he had gone to join a shooting party.

" (Swythamley Park, Macclesfield, 11/12/04.)

"I have been away from England this autumn hunting Moose and Caribou in the wilds of the Yukon Territory, but on my return home last month I found two of your letters awaiting me and I got the third the other day. I assure you they have interested me very much indeed, as well as some of your letters to the *Field* which I have also seen.

" With the exception of Caribou, which, when on migration, go in enormous herds, game in the wilds of Northern Canada is very scarce and scattered when compared with African game. We were in a very wild and little known country this year, where there were no Indians, and no white hunters, with the exception of a few trappers who shoot very little, and do not go into the mountains at all, where we were, but we found game very scarce.

" I shot four bull moose, and might have shot four more, but they had not good heads.

"One of my moose carried a truly magnificent head. [Selous afterwards sent me a photograph of this trophy.—D.D.L.] It will be the finest trophy in my collection. It has 41 points, and measures 5 feet 6 inches across the palms. A second head measures 4 feet 10½ inches.

"Besides the moose I only saw three Caribou, and got one good head, and a good many white sheep, but they were all ewes and lambs. The rams were by themselves and we could not find them.

"I am now using a ·375 bore rifle by Holland, but I don't think it is any better for all ordinary game than my old ·303 which got worn out.

"I don't think I shall ever visit the part of Africa where you have been shooting lately, as I have already got all the animals that can be got anywhere in Northern Rhodesia, except the Situtunga, which I have never yet shot. If I go to Africa again I shall go to some part of East or West Africa, where there are species of antelopes quite new to me. I have already made one trip to East Africa, and got several species there which are not to be found in South Africa.

"I am glad you have succeeded in shooting some good elephant bulls. The one shot by Mr. Melland, the Native Commissioner, with tusks weighing 119½ and 117 pounds is certainly one of the finest ever shot by a European. Oswell shot one whose tusks weighed 250 pounds the two, and Neumann has shot some with tusks nearly 120 pounds each.

Lately a Mr. Butter shot one on the borders of Abyssinia with tusks weighing 135 and 138 pounds. I saw these tusks at Ward's, and understood from him that Mr. Butter had shot the elephant they had orginally belonged to himself. An elephant was shot three years ago by two Germans on Kilimanjaro, in East Africa, with tusks weighing a little over 120 pounds each. I saw these tusks myself at Voi, in East Africa. They were a beautiful, long, even pair.

"When you come to England you must be sure and come and see me, and then we can have a good talk about our travels and hunting adventures. I am getting old, and cannot get away for anything but short trips now. Wishing you good health and good luck.

(Signed) " F. C. SELOUS."

Then comes an interesting letter mentioning who shot the specimen of the White Rhinoceros now in the Cape Town Museum.

" (Heatherside, Worplesdon, 19/1/06.)
" I have to thank you for your very interesting letter of Novr. 14th which I duly received some time ago, and would have answered before this, but I have been very busy lately going about England giving lectures. I put myself in the hands of a lecture agency, and they get engagements for me. It is rather a strain, but brings in a good bit of

money, and it is easier to make money by lecturing than by writing. As I lecture on my hunting experiences in Africa long ago I am still making money out of my hunting.

"I have been looking out for your article in the *Field*, but it has not yet appeared. I shall read it with great interest when it comes out.

"I am much interested to learn that you have killed all your elephants with a ·303 rifle. [This was before I shot others with Mannlicher and Mauser rifles.—D.D.L.] Really these small bore rifles are wonderful. Did you shoot your elephants in the head, or kill them with body shots in the heart and lungs ?

"I am quite sure that the White Rhinoceros in the Cape Town Museum was shot and preserved by Mr. Arthur Eyre, but he may have sold it to Mr. Harvey Brown, who sold it to Rhodes, who gave it to the Cape Town Museum. Eyre was with Coryndon in 1892 when he shot the first white rhino he preserved (the skin of which I think went bad). The next year, in 1893, Coryndon went by himself and shot and preserved two bulls, one of which is in the British Museum at South Kensington, and the other in Rothschild's Museum at Tring. The next year, 1894, Eyre went to the same district and shot the bull now in the Cape Museum.

"When I was in Salisbury, in July, 1895, I saw the skin and skull, with a very good horn, of this specimen, and heard all about it.

"Harvey Brown, to the best of my belief, never

saw a white rhino in the flesh, but he shot and preserved a black one. He may have bought the white one now in the Cape Museum and so got his name on it.

" I am afraid there is not much to be done in the way of getting orders for specimens of African animals for museums. I got the cream of this work and made over £2,000, minus expenses, by it, but now all the museums in England are full, and the Americans are sending out their own collectors.

" Wishing you good health and good luck, and hoping to see you here one of these days.

(Signed) " F. C. SELOUS."

Next comes a short letter about a piece of wood which came from the tree Dr. David Livingstone's heart was buried under at Chitambo's village, N.E. Rhodesia.

" (Heatherside, Worplesdon, 7/7/06.)

" Thanks very much for the piece of wood from the tree under which Dr. Livingstone's heart was buried.

" I am most fearfully busy getting all my things together for my trip to the Yukon.

" I enclose the only photo I have at the moment of my big moose head.

" I am glad the *Field* people are pleased with my little introduction to your book. I think I was quite right to put men like yourself and Capt.

Stigand, and I may add myself, in quite a different class to the very rich men who go to Africa for a very short trip because it is the fashion, and who manage to get a few big game heads with the help of their Somali hunters, but who, if they were put down in Africa without anyone to help, would not be capable of finding and killing game by themselves. Once more wishing you the best of luck.

(Signed) " F. C. SELOUS."

Then follows a letter dated March 3rd, 1907, from Heatherside, telling me about his last Yukon trip, when he got six caribou with fine heads, the best specimen with horns of fifty-seven inches being mounted complete for the Natural History Museum in South Kensington.   This was to be placed alongside a Newfoundland caribou of his, also mounted entire.   He also mentions a moose with fine horns spreading sixty-three inches, and two wolves—one with a beautiful black-coloured skin.

Now comes a very long and interesting letter :

" (Heatherside, November 18th, 1909.)

" It is too bad of me never to have written to you all this time, especially as you have been so good as to write me several very interesting letters.   The success of my trip to East Africa was, to a considerable extent, marred by rain and long grass on the Gwas N'gishu plateau, near Mount Elgon, which was the best game country for lions I was in.   The lions on this high plateau (8,000 feet above sea level) often grow really magnificent manes, and I was very anxious to get a chance at one, but before the grass got long I had no luck, and never saw one at all, and when we got to the N'zoia river, where there were a great many lions about, the grass was 6 feet high near the river, and nowhere less than 4 feet high, and it was quite impossible to see a lion at all.

" I was over three months in the Veld hunting altogether and never got a chance of a shot at a lion, although one day, on our return journey, I saw two lionesses and galloped them, but there was a lot of bush in full leaf and the grass was rather long too, and they crouched and disappeared suddenly when I was close on to them, and as the spoor afterwards showed I galloped past within seven yards of where one of them was lying. Judd (the man who was managing the caravan) was following me and about 80 yards behind, and when he got near one of the lionesses she charged at him at close quarters.

"Judd's horse reared up and swung round and Judd fell off, but as he did so he pulled off his rifle, holding it across his thighs. By a marvellous piece of luck the bullet went right into the lioness's eye, killing it instantly, and Judd lay on the ground alongside the dead lioness.

" Although we had so much rain on the Gwas N'gishu plateau there was a very severe drought over the greater part of the country, and all round the Athi Plains and near Nairobi the country was parched up and there was no grass at all. With the exception of lions and elephants—which we had expected to meet with near Mount Elgon, but did not come across—I got all the kinds of game to be got in the countries I was in, and shot altogether 104 head—most of them for meat for our porters.

" The species I got were Rhino, Giraffe, Eland, Oryx, Jackson's Wildebeest, Jackson's Hartebeest, Coke's Hartebeest, Topi, Waterbuck (Defassa), Uganda Kob, Bohor Reedbuck, Chanler's Reedbuck, Impala, Grant's and Thomson's Gazelles, Oribi (Cotton's), Steinbuck and Duiker. Also Serval and Colobus monkey. I saw four leopards, but only got just a glimpse of three of them. The fourth came out of the long grass near the N'zoia river and stood in full view on the sloping trunk of a big tree. I had an excellent chance at it at about 200 yards, but I am sorry to say missed. I also saw several chetahs on the open plains, but did not gallop after them as I did not want to take it out of my horse too much. I had a splendid gallop after two 5-horned giraffe bulls I shot (one for myself and one for my host, Mr. McMillan).

" Of course, this trip was made at the wrong time of year—the rainy season—and I knew that before I started, but as I went out as Mr. McMillan's guest and free of all expense I had to go then or not at all.

" Fortunately for Mr. Roosevelt no rain to speak of fell in the country in which he was hunting during the first three months of his trip, so there was no long grass or heavy dew to trouble him. I daresay you have seen in the papers something about one of our party having been mauled by a lion. That was a Mr. Williams, McMillan's secretary. He and I were hunting together for a month before McMillan joined us, and during that time he had the luck to come on first a lioness, and later on a lion, both of which he got. The lion was a very large one, but without much mane, and I must have disturbed it, though I never saw it. I had left Williams with the horses and all the boys, and was going after some Oryx with one Somali. This was about 2 p.m., and very hot, and we must have disturbed the lion, as it walked right on to where Williams was sitting with all the boys and the horses, and he shot it from where he sat.

" Later, on the first day, after we had passed the farms that have been taken up on the Gwas N'gishu plateau, Williams had a little too much luck, as he walked right on to another lion, and slightly wounding it at about 200 yards, it came straight for him. He fired at it as it came on with his double ·450, and missed it with the right barrel, and only grazed it with the left, and it then got him by the calf of the leg and bit him badly, and would no doubt have killed him had it not been for his Swahili boy who carried his small rifle, and who stood by him and fired two or three shots into the lion, which then let go of Williams and lay down close-to dying.

" Williams then got hold of his rifle and, putting another cartridge in, fired into the lion and killed it.

" Williams has had a very bad time and almost lost his leg, though we sent him off to Nairobi—he had to be carried on a stretcher five days to the nearest point on the railway—the next day. He is now in a private hospital in London, and it will be a long time before he recovers the use of his leg.

" Well, that's all I can tell you about my trip, if you have had patience to read it all.

" No doubt you would enjoy a trip to the Yukon, but it would not do to try and make a living there by trapping after all the years you have spent in Africa. I am just off to America myself as I am very worried about some investments I have out there, and I cannot get any really reliable information about them in this country. I am starting for New York (without my rifle) on Saturday, Novr. 27th, and hope to get back early in January next. It is a beastly nuisance having to go, but I think it is the best thing to do.

" And now I must close. Please write to me from time to time even though I do not always answer your letters at once, as it always interests me so much to hear from you.

" Hoping to see you when you next come to England, and wishing you the best of luck and a merry Christmas and some good bull elephants.

(Signed) " F. C. SELOUS."

Then the next interesting letter dated July 17th, 1910, discusses the habits of tsetse flies and rhinos, and he sent me the copies of two letters he had sent to the *Field* and *Times* about tsetse.

On November 21st, 1910, he again writes me this letter :

" Your letter of Sept. 9th reached me some time ago and I enjoyed reading it very much.

" I have been reading your book lately, and to me at least it is very interesting as I know that you are a very careful observer, and that every word you write is correct. [Here follow even more complimentary remarks which I refrain from giving.— D.D.L.]

" I am afraid that you cannot hope to make much money by a book on sport and natural history in any part of Africa, as so many books have been published lately on such subjects in different parts of Africa that it is impossible that all of them can have a good sale. No doubt Mr. Roosevelt's book will sell well, and it is a good and interesting book in itself, but that is not the reason it will sell, which is because it was written by a great and well-known personality. Somewhere in this book Mr. Roosevelt refers to my last book, *African Nature Notes and Reminiscences*, and praises it, but, good or bad, it met with no appreciation in this country, only had a very limited sale, and is now quite forgotten. I really think one can make more money by writing articles for the —— and —— and magazines than by writing books.

" I am going to the Sudan after all this winter after the Giant Elands. The Natural History Museum are very anxious to get specimens of these animals whilst it is still possible to do so, and the trustees have voted me a grant of —— to help to defray the expenses of my trip, and this vote has now been passed by the Treasury so I am going, and shall leave England on Jan. 20th. Of course I shall have letters from the Foreign Office to the Sudan Government, and I expect they will not require me to take out a game licence, and will give me a free passage on the Government steamer from Khartoum to Gondokoro.

"I expect to get all facilities granted me as I shall be engaged on work for the Museum, and if so my expenses will be very much less than they would be if I went out on my own.

"Walter Rothschild also wants me to bring him a complete specimen of a big bull of the Giant Eland, and a few other things, for which altogether he offers me ——, so that altogether I hope to do the trip at only a small expense to myself. I am not sure, however, that I shall be able to get a permit to shoot an extra Eland for Rothschild. My worst enemy will be 'Anno Domini,' as on Decr. 31st I shall be 59 years old, and as I am going down to the Lado (of which Stigand is now in charge), where it is excessively hot I am told, and the climate rather bad, I may not be able to stand the work. If I can only keep fairly well I shall have a most interesting trip.

"The Museum want a specimen of a Northern White Rhinoceros, and if I can get the elands pretty quickly near Redjaf (where Mr. Roosevelt got his) I shall try for one a little further up the Nile. But the preservation of the skin will be the trouble, as the whole skin will, I believe, have to be pared down, and I shall have no one to help me but a few raw savages.

" I hope you will get a good male Inyala to add to your collection. They are, I think, one of the handsomest of African antelopes.

" By the bye, a new antelope has lately been discovered by two young fellows on a shooting trip in the mountains on the borders of Abyssinia (9,000 feet above sea level). It is as big (the male) as a Koodoo cow, with horns which spread nearly as broad as a Koodoo's, but are only about half as long, no beard under the throat, but white chest and throat patches, as in the Lesser Koodoo, uniform dark brown in colour, with no stripes in one specimen, and two or three in another, and in both half a dozen white spots in a line along the side and on the haunch. It is quite a new and distinct species, in some ways like a Koodoo, in others more like a mountain Situtunga or an Inyala.

" The sleeping sickness seems to be spreading everywhere, and to be getting more and more dangerous for Europeans. I had a long and very interesting talk with Sir David Bruce the other day about the various species of tsetse flies, and he told me that 17 Germans are now on their way home from Lake Tanganyika, all of whom have got sleeping sickness germs in their blood. I suppose you have heard that several cases of sleeping sickness have lately occurred in the Valley of the Luangwa, 400 miles from the nearest point where Glossina palpalis is found. This seems to show that some

species of tsetse other than ' palpalis ' can carry the
trypanosome of sleeping sickness. I hope it will
prove to be ' fusca,' or anything but ' morsitans,'
as if the latter can be proved to be capable of carrying
the germ of sleeping sickness an attempt may be
made to get rid of it by killing-off all game, even
in ' fly ' districts which are altogether unsuitable for
every kind of colonization.

"Now goodbye, and wishing you the best of
luck, and with all good wishes for Christmas and
the New Year.

(Signed) " F. C. SELOUS."

The remarks by Selous on the sleeping sickness I
received when I was busy having a long controversy
in the *Nyasaland Times* about killing off the game
because some thought it formed a " host " for the
sleeping-sickness germ. All practical hunters know
that one often sees game where there are no tsetse
flies, and plenty of the flies where game is absent
or very scarce indeed. Although tsetse are blood
feeders, it is my firm belief that they also eat vegetable
matter. Besides the game animals they also bite
monkeys and other small creatures. This is a subject
which is not yet settled, and would take too long to
discuss here, though it is sufficient to remark that if
ever the game is exterminated on such false grounds
it can never reduce the number of tsetse flies.
Therefore, the extirpation of the game would be a
senseless crime.

The next letter I shall quote is penned from
Heatherside, Worplesdon, Surrey, and dated October
1st, 1911.

" My Dear Lyell,

" I have just got your letter of Aug. 12th and I
am just writing these few lines in acknowledgment.
I hope you got my letters with enclosures which I
sent to the address your father gave me.

" I think I told you all about the operation I had
to undergo. I got over it very well indeed and am
now perfectly fit and well again. I am going with
W. N. MacMillan to East Africa again in December.

" I don't like the open plains country myself, but
we are going, I believe, down the Northern Gwas
N'yiro river to the Lorian Swamp, and that will be
all bush country, I think. MacMillan has asked me
to be his guest on this trip from London to London,
and, as if I don't go with him someone else will, I
had no hesitation in accepting his invitation.

" I think I had fair cause of complaint in the
Sudan. I never intended to go to the Bahr-el-
Ghazal at all. I obtained special leave through Sir
E. Grey and the Trustees of the British Museum to
go into the Lado Enclave from Redjaf to the place
where Roosevelt got the elands—a very easy and
inexpensive journey as it is only 30 miles from the
Nile. I made all my arrangements for this trip,
but when I got to Khartoum I found that an
Austrian who had come out to get one of the
Sudanese elands for the Vienna Museum had been
sent to this place just ahead of me, and as there is
only one water-hole there I would not follow him,
and had to fit out a very expensive trip to the centre
of the Bahr-el-Ghazal Province. I was unlucky,

too, in getting that heavy thunderstorm on the only day I saw the elands.

" I had a letter to the Sirdar from the Trustees of the Museum and put it into his hands myself, but I was never able to see him afterwards, though he made an appointment which he did not keep. He absolutely ignored me and did nothing whatever to help me.

" I may, however, go to the Bahr-el-Ghazal again, as Capt. Feilden, the Governor of the Province, has promised to help me if I can manage to do so, but next time I will just go as a private individual and ask no favours from the high officials of the Sudan.

These Sudanese elands are uncertain animals to get, as, if disturbed, they are given to moving long distances into waterless country where they can't be followed. Much of the country they frequent, too, is very thick, so that it is difficult to get a sight of a good one.

" Nyasaland now seems a first rate country for a shooting trip, and your forthcoming book ought to be very useful to anyone who contemplates going there. I shall look forward to reading it, but I am afraid it will not be out before I leave for East Africa.

" I fear, however, that you cannot hope to make much out of it, but the orders from the ——— Museum ought to keep you going for some time to come. I hope they will give you good prices for your specimens.

"Now goodbye, and wishing you the very best
of luck and good health.
        "Believe me,
            "Yours very truly,
                (Signed) "F. C. SELOUS."

Selous, in nearly all his letters to me, concluded
them in the same way, and seldom varied his ending
of : "Believe me, Yours very truly "; and I believe
this was his habit with all the letters to his friends.

In the Sudan trip described above there is no doubt
that the Sudan high officials treated him badly and
with discourtesy. Selous himself was one of the
most courteous men who ever lived, and if the saying
that "Manners makyth man" is correct there was
no finer man than he, for he was the soul of
politeness and straightness.

Then a letter written from Heatherside, and
dated May 30th, 1912 :

"I have just returned home from East Africa. I
have been away over five months and was four
months in the country. We had quite an interesting
trip, passing over the shoulder of Mount Kenia,
then down the Northern Gwas N'yiro river which
we followed to the Lorian Swamp.

"On the voyage home I wrote up an account of
our trip from my diary, and if the *Field* publishes it
you will see it, as you take in that paper, so I won't
attempt to tell you much about it, as I am very busy
just now. However, although I met with certain

disappointments, on the other hand I got several
new things for my collection—Lesser Koodoo,
Gerunuk, Oryx Beisa, Grevy's Zebra, Somali
Reticulated Giraffe, Striped Hyæna, three kinds of
Dik-Diks, and a Zanzibar Suni.

" I also got two buffalo bulls—all one is allowed to
shoot. I have seen and been much interested in all
your letters to the *Field*.

" It was an awful pity that you were not able to
preserve that magnificent Eland. He must have
been a splendid specimen, and it is very interesting
to me to have your careful measurements showing
that Elands do sometimes attain a standing height of
six feet at the withers. I have only measured a
small number of the big bulls I shot in Mashonaland,
and the tallest of these was 5 ft. 10 ins. at the wither,
though, of course, there may have been taller animals
amongst the many old bulls which I did not measure.

" I quite agree with all you say as to the relative
danger of photographing and shooting dangerous
animals.   Mr. —— took some beautiful photographs,
but you will notice that he makes out that every
rhino he saw was charging, or just going to charge,
when, with one exception, it is evident that none of
the rhinos he photographed was charging.

" I am afraid I shan't be able to get out to Africa
again for some time, if ever, which is a nuisance, as
I wanted to have another try after the Sudan eland
next winter.

" We were in very hot country along the Gwas
N'yiro river as it is less than one degree north of the

Equator, and only 1,200 to 1,500 feet above sea
level.

"However, I stood the climate very well, and
was not only fit and well all the time, but able to
do really a lot of walking. Now goodbye for the
present and hoping to hear from you again before
long and trusting you are keeping well, and have
been getting some good things, and gathering interesting material for more writing.
                    (Signed) " F. C. SELOUS."

Then, in a letter from Heatherside written on
July 30th, 1911, Selous seems to have forgotten that
he wrote me on November 18th, 1909, an account of
Williams's mauling by a lion, as he repeats much of
this account, as well as the account of Judd's narrow
shave.

It is so interesting, however, and other points
crop up, that I give the letter :

"Your father is coming down to see us to-day.
I have already heard from him that you could not
get on with the people with whom you went to
B.E.A., and that you have returned to B.C.A.
But with a good horse on those open plains in
East Africa what a bag of lions one could make!!
Both times I have been out there I have been unlucky.
The first time I hadn't got a horse, and as it rained
all the time I was there, and the grass was very long
on the plains round Nairobi, I never saw a lion.
Two years ago, when I went with W. N. Mac-

Millan to the Gwas N'gishu plateau, in June and July, it again rained all the time, and the grass soon got so long that, although there were any number of lions along the N'zoia river, it was impossible to do anything with them.

" Our companion, Williams, got charged and bitten soon after we had passed Sirgoit Hill, and the only lions I saw at all were two lionesses which I galloped in the longish grass. The one I was close behind squatted suddenly behind a bush and let me pass within seven yards, as the tracks afterwards showed, and she then charged Judd who was coming on a good way behind me. He had a most miraculous escape, as the lioness charged when he was quite close. His horse reared up and swung round, and Judd fell off and landed on his shoulders. As he fell he told me he pulled off his rifle in the lioness's face when it was almost touching the horse, and his bullet went right into its right eye, and when he recovered from his fall he found it lying dead alongside of him. I caught his horse and brought it back to him, and examined all the tracks, and as far as I can see Judd's story is quite true.

" I should have written to you long ago, but soon after coming home from the Sudan, as a result of an examination by a specialist, I had to undergo a rather bad operation. For years past apparently, although I had never suffered in any way from it, my —— —— had been enlarged, and as the specialist said that sooner or later I would have to undergo an operation, and the sooner the better as

I was now in very good health, I decided to have it at once.

" I had a damned great hole cut in my guts, right into the ——, and the —— removed. I have made, they say, a wonderful recovery—the record recovery, they said at the Home I was in in London—and I simply healed up like a dog, or a savage, but of course, I have to go slowly for a bit yet.

" I am sending you herewith the account I wrote of my trip to the Bahr-el-Ghazal which you may not have seen in the *Field*.

" MacMillan has asked me to go with him at the end of December to East Africa again and I have agreed to go. He wants to go down the Northern Gwas N'yro river, to the Lorian Swamp. It ought to be a very nice trip. My eyesight keeps wonderfully good, but I can no longer shoot as well as I used to do. I am unsteady and I can't make out quite why. But I no longer shoot well enough to take many risks with lions.

" I was most awfully sorry to hear of poor George Grey's death. I have known him very well for many years and he was one of the best fellows in the world.

" I hope your book is selling, but I know how small the sale for books on African hunting is now as there are so many, and the bad ones spoil the sale of the good ones. Your book appealed to me, just for the same reason that my books appeal to you, because we both know what we are writing about, and each of us knows that everything stated by the other is right.

" Wishing you the best of good luck, and hoping to see you when you again come home.

(Signed) " F. C. SELOUS."

In the above letter Selous, when mentioning his severe operation, uses the expression about having " healed up like a dog." He did the same when writing to other of his friends for J. G. Millais in his *Life of Frederick Courtenay Selous, D.S.O.*, mentions the same phrase.

The remarks on the late Mr. George Grey show how much he was thought of. In Northern Rhodesia I have heard men say that George Grey was one of the finest Englishmen who ever lived in Africa. He was killed by a lion when hunting in B.E.A. with Sir Alfred Pease. It charged him, and he hit it full in the face with a ·280 Ross rifle, but the bullet went into chips and failed to penetrate, with the consequence that he succumbed to his severe injuries. George Grey had a brother Charles, whom I met in Zomba, Nyasaland, in 1903. He, like George Grey, was a splendid fellow, who fought in the war and lost an arm. This did not make him stop hunting as he was eventually killed by a buffalo he had wounded.

The adventurous lives of these two fine brothers, and the reputations they made in wilder Africa, show how breeding tells in the unconventional places of the earth, for there character alone counts.

Now I come to the last of his letters, and may say that I have only given copies of about half the letters I kept which he wrote to me from 1898 to 1914.

" (Heatherside, Worplesdon, Surrey, 14/8/1914.)

"When this war broke out, I felt that it was a life and death struggle, not only for Germany and France, but also for Great Britain, as if the Germans were to beat France and our Army and impose terms they would take Belgium, Holland and the north-west corner of France, and eventually smash us, so I felt that I ought to offer my services for what they might be worth.

"I first went to a large life insurance office in London, and was examined by their chief medical officer, who found that every organ in my body was sound, and certified that, in his opinion, I was fit for any kind of active service, so I then went and offered myself to Colonel Driscoll, who will be in command of 'A' or Expeditionary Force of the Legion of Frontiersmen. I have now been enrolled in this force, and Col. Driscoll has promised that where he goes I go, either as Intelligence Officer or Troop Leader. I am no good for going into a camp and really doing nothing, for, like you, I can't stand drill, and don't think for a moment that the Germans will ever send a raiding force to the east coast of England or Scotland. It may be weeks or months before the Government employ any irregular forces, but sooner or later they may have to do so.

"With all good wishes and hoping to see you again should you ever come south.

(Signed) " F. C. SELOUS."

As everyone knows this fine man fell in action in German East Africa on January 4th, 1917, exactly a year before his elder son, Fred, who, as Capt. F. H. B. Selous, M.C., was killed in an air combat in France on the same date as his father, but a year later.

On March 15th, 1906, when home from Africa, I stayed with Selous at Heatherside, near Worplesdon, and on a later occasion met his son Fred who was at Rugby. He was a very fine youngster, and had he lived would have been a man like his father. I am sure had the son fallen first it would have cut him up greatly, as judging from some remarks he made to me when going round his trophies in his museum, I think he hoped his elder boy would emulate his own deeds in the hunting-fields of Africa.

Ever since I read his first book, *A Hunter's Wanderings in Africa*, published in 1881 by Richard Bentley & Son, I admired him, for I instinctively knew that he was a man of the truth. No flowery language, but matter-of-fact observations on the wild game of Africa. That volume went with me in all my hunting trips, and I have read it from cover to cover more times than I can remember. Perhaps his *African Nature Notes and Reminiscences* is better written, but I think his first work by far the best.

I remember how he smiled when he showed me his old 4 bore Roer with which he shot many of his first elephants and other game as we went over his fine museum. Later, in his study, he also showed me a ·375 single Holland, and a ·256 Mannlicher he had in a cabinet and remarked : " Had I only had one of these rifles in my early days I would have shot thrice the number of elephants I did." In this room he had a great collection of birds' eggs very neatly arranged.

I shall always treasure the letters of his I kept, and also a signed photograph he sent me when I was in the African bush, as well as a signed catalogue of the specimens in his museum. He also gave me a photograph of his big Yukon moose head which he considered the best trophy he ever shot.

Selous had a wonderful charm of manner, and very straight blue eyes, and was certainly one of the finest men of his time ; in fact it is doubtful whether we shall ever see his like again, for the conditions which enabled him to be as he was are passing away, if they have not already gone for ever.

This inventive age may have its advantages and its comforts, but the use of motor cars and aeroplanes will never tend to make men as manly as they were in the days when they had to depend wholly on their own physical powers of hardihood ; nor can it produce that spirit of adventure which, in men like Selous, did so much to form our splendid Empire.

CHAPTER II

Major C. H. Stigand, O.B.E., R. J. Cuninghame, M.C.,
T. A. Barns and Capt. Martin Ryan

THE first time I met the late Major C. H. Stigand was in Zomba, Nyasaland, in 1903, when I got an appointment at "The Camp," the Boma of the King's African Rifles. Here I had as quarters a nice brick house with glass windows and a cool thatched roof, and this was the only " pukka " house I dwelt in during the years I lived in South Central Africa.

Besides Stigand other officers at " The Camp " I remember were Capt. J. P. Ll. Mostyn, Capt. Markham, Capt. McLeod and Capt. J. W. S. Wingfield-Digby.

Stigand, Mostyn and Digby often took week-end shooting trips some twenty to thirty miles into the surrounding country and at various times I accompanied one or the other, when we usually had some sport and a cheery time until we had to get back to work.

At that time there was still a good lot of game left within the radius mentioned, and on the occasions I went up Zomba Mountain, where fine views could be got, and also a shot at bushbuck sometimes, it was a fair shooting country. On several occasions I have seen the spoor of elephants on the plateau of

Zomba Mountain, and once the tracks of a rhinoceros. Now, I believe, there are trout in the streams flowing from the mountain.

In the country beyond Namitembo there were then eland, koodoo, sable, Lichtenstein's hartebeest, bushbuck, reedbuck, oribi, duiker, zebra, warthog, bushpig, etc., and there was always the possibility of getting a chance at lion and leopard.

Lions even visited " The Camp," and one night a hungry lion broke into a goat-house and killed several of these animals and a calf, but he did not live long after this escapade, as I now own his skull and skin.

Then I resigned my billet at " The Camp " and went off and hunted elephants round Fort Manning and at the same time collected drawings of spoor and made notes for a book which Stigand and I brought out in 1906. These meetings at the Fort with Stigand and Mostyn I look back on with great pleasure, as they were both the best of fellows.

Soon afterwards I went to North-Eastern Rhodesia, the adjacent territory to Nyasaland, and soon after getting there I went west to the Loangwa River to hunt, and lived in a wattle and daub hut at a place called Mzazas. When I was there Stigand wrote me that he had had a mix-up with a rhino, and besides other injuries it had gored him deeply in the chest, just over the heart. His battalion of the 1st King's African Rifles had been ordered for service in British East Africa, and before Stigand's wounds had properly healed he walked the whole distance to Zomba with the troops. Here he sent me an account of his scrap with the rhino :

" (Zomba, Nyasaland, 11/6/1905.)

" We are off in a few days. Sorry I haven't been able to write. I have been so beastly busy as I have had to push all the recruits through musketry. Hope you are fit and well again, so sorry to hear you had been seedy.

" Marabouts are white and black—bareheaded, yellow beaks, very long. [This was about an old discussion.—D.D.L.]

" I shall probably be going home on leave from Mombasa in about two months so try and buck-up with the other things. I will try and get gnu spoor there. [He sometimes sent me rough sketches to finish.—D.D.L.] Re rhino, they both went for me at once without any provocation. I put a bullet into one's head at point blank range. [Here follows a rough sketch of the spot where he was charged.—D.D.L.] You will notice by diagram that it wasn't a blind rush up-wind or a blind charge. I think they had heard me, and they galloped round a bit and then came diving through a clump of grass one yard from me when I thought they had galloped off, and finally, after one of them had rolled me along the ground, and then turned round and come back to toss me, he went off in the direction he originally came from. Needless to say I was delighted to see his old wrinkled bottom going off !

" When I found my rifle, etc., we heard him again either come back, or the one I hit perhaps had fallen down and was getting up again. I was, of course, too bad to go and see as my chest was laid open, and

I wasn't quite sure whether it had got the lungs or not, and waited rather anxiously to see if I spat blood. It also missed the heart by about an $\frac{1}{8}$th of an inch, and the wonderful part was it did not break a rib.

" Let us try and get this book off soon or it will hang on forever.

(Signed) " C. H. STIGAND."

Stigand had a marvellous shave from death with the rhino and he was soon to have an almost narrower one with a lion. When he got to Simba (Swahili word for lion.—D.D.L.), on the Uganda Railway, he heard that lions were coming to drink the water which formed a small pool under a tank near the station, so he got leave to stop and sit up for them. He killed three, but one was only wounded, which he followed at night into thick grass. It knocked him down so that he could not use his Mannlicher, so he punched it with his right fist and it left him. It seems he was hitting it where his first bullet had smashed its lower jaw, a fact which saved his life.

He was taken to Nairobi, where good treatment saved his life, as he nearly died of blood-poisoning. For years afterwards he had a stiff arm, as the ligaments and nerves had been badly damaged. I saw the three skins and skulls afterwards in London, and he was there getting treatment and told me the whole story of one of the most thrilling experiences a man ever had at night with lions.

On his way home he wrote me the following letter :

" (Mombasa Club, East Africa, 19/9/05.)

"How are you? I have been able to do nothing here as for the first month we were at a beastly place called Mazeras with no game, and everybody was sick, and the last month I have been in hospital at Nairobi, the result of shooting lions, my first day's shoot in this country. I am off home on six months' leave now.

"Try and send me the spoor that remains to be done if you can. We had better leave this country out as I have, of course, been able to do nothing. My address at home is [Here follows a name and address.—D.D.L.]. I told you that I wouldn't lose faith in my Mannlicher till I had been mauled by a lion. Now I have modified my opinion. A small bore is still what I shall shoot with for all the reasons given in that well-known work : —— —— —— —— —— ——, i.e., light to carry, magazine, light cartridges, more accurate, especially for shooting standing, cheaper, etc. etc. BUT for a springing or charging lion (wounded) and for the violent animals at very close quarters one wants a 15 pounder, or large bore howitzer; or 12 inch wire gun would be safer. The difficulty is how to exchange your small bore for a large at the critical moment.

"I am going all round the gunmakers and will study the question.

"I shall be several months before I shall be able to use my left arm properly again, and perhaps shall have to have an operation at home.

" I have heard a lot about lions, and have come to the conclusion that following a wounded lion into grass is two or three to one on the lion!

" Hope you are fit. Excuse this scrawl, awful hurry as I have just decided to go home by first boat and getting everything ready.

(Signed) " C. H. STIGAND."

Stigand's remarks on small-bore rifles were meant as a joke, as he continued to use his ·256 Mannlicher, and shot a number of lions and other game with it after his narrow escape. No rifle of whatever bore can be absolutely certain to stop a charging lion, for unless the bullet brains it, or breaks the spine, it may have the strength and courage to come on. Even a shot in the lower part of the heart might not down it, though one through the top of that organ would probably cause almost instant paralysis of the nervous system.

He wrote next from London, where he was undergoing treatment for his crippled arm. Massage in the course of time made a considerable improvement in the damaged nerves and ligaments.

On returning to British East he wrote :

" (Fort Hall, B.E. Africa, 21/8/07.)

" Received yours of 23/6/07. What a long time letters take between these ruddy places.

" I am waiting to hear result of last half yearly accounts to write and urge on them to buck-up with the 2nd Edition while the Big Game hobby is still on and before all the big game has been shot. The book is practically no good for the beggars that come to this country as they come to shoot a few common heads in the Athi Plains at long range, and don't trouble about anything that wants hunting. However, a lot of them bring a copy and go back home thinking that they are expert hunters!

" I heard of two fellows who were in Uganda (a thick country) shooting, and they said that it was of the greatest service to them. Therefore, as soon as you see how the sales go last June, if favourable send on the photos and notes to me and I shall reforward them to your governor, together with mine which, I am afraid, will not be much.

" I may come home with 1/K.A.R. in March, in which case I will trek up through N.E. Rhodesia.

" Try and get tenders for Bongo skin and bones. Okapi, ditto, and live of both animals, and then we will know what we are at. It is no good bringing a silly looking animal like an Okapi alive all the way to the coast and then finding he fetches £50. I will write to Rothschild. Also birds. I did not know partridge were so easy to catch. I have been in camp about three days here and we have noosed about 15 partridges. I should think that any bird that eats anything you can supply it with ought to be catchable.

(Signed) " C. H. STIGAND."

The part about bongo and okapi referred to some idea we had of going to the Congo to try and

catch specimens of these fairly rare animals. Judging
from information we got later, this would have been
a puzzle, for it is hard enough to get a shot at these
creatures which is infinitely easier than catching
them alive.

The next letter is, I see, written from :

" (Nairobi, B.E. Africa. 8/12/07.)

" Just a line to keep up to date. That 2nd Edn.
seems a long time coming.

" I have just come up from an unknown part of
the Tana river. Got 3 lion, all ♂, and 1 cheetah ♀.
Latter had two ribs across back of his hind pad
which would tend to make the finger marks as in
illustration. I took 5 photos so one should come
out. I was surprised to see that the claws were just
like a dog's. I must study the spoor when I get a
chance. The lion were all sporting finishes. All
moving shots at long range except one, which was
close-by, but moving, and cold dark morning before
sunrise. Result was that all were only wounded
by first shot. One, a tawny-maned, went into a
thick patch of thorn, where I followed, and he
fortunately growled and showed where he was.
One, a black-maned, went into a cave and I went in
after him and found him dead. When I tried to
pull him out in the dark I found he had no tail, only
a sore stump (trap or croc ?).

" The third, a red-maned, I was looking for when
suddenly heard him moving in a very thick bit of

watercourse. He tried to break cover, but I hit him again in shoulder and he went back.

"Then it took a devil of a job throwing stones, etc. When a stone hit him he only growled. At last, when a big stone hit him, he moved down into the bottom of the watercourse where it was thinner. I went to the edge and looked through the bushes and he tried to *spring out, but fell back as his shoulder was broken, and I finished him. Best luck.
(Signed) " C. H. STIGAND."

" PS.—*For ' spring out ' read ' jink out ! ' "

The asterisk as PS. was a joke as I used to talk about a man or animal doing a " jink." This word is used in India about pig-sticking, and one says a pig jinks when it dodges aside. Stigand always said there was no such word, and I argued there was, and it was a useful one to describe a quick dodge. I have just looked it up in Chambers's *Twentieth Century Dictionary*, and I see it is a Scottish word meaning " to move nimbly," " to elude," and so on. Being a Scottish word I see now why my friend thought it non-existent.

The letter describes some narrow squeaks, but he does not tell the full story of the lion in the cave. Afterwards he told me that when the animal disappeared into the cavern, which was dark, his cook, who was with him, in bravado said he would go in when Stigand naturally thought of leaving it there for a time. To show the natives that a white man was " not backward in coming forward " Stigand, much against his common sense, went in, and as he

MARTIN RYAN

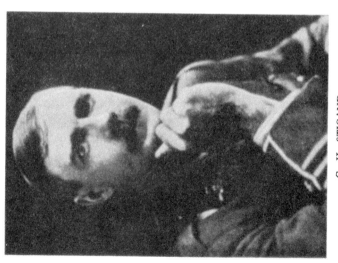

C. H. STIGAND

remarks found the beast defunct. I think that instead of losing its caudal appendage by a trap or croc it had probably been mauled in a fight with another male, and got its tail bitten off in the scrimmage, or had it so severely chewed that it had recently rotted off.

Considering Stigand had not long before been badly mauled by a lion near Simba, not to mention his severe injuries from the rhino, it shows how plucky he was in taking such grave risks. It is all very well beginners being reckless through ignorance, but he was a man of great experience and knowledge, so this proves how resolute he was as a hunter.

He went off to the Congo Free State to shoot elephant and wanted me to do a few sketches of spoor for his new book, *The Game of British East Africa*, which I soon completed and sent. He afterwards, when the book came out, sent me a copy which I still have. In it will be found much information on the East African game, though I do not quite agree with what he says about splitting up the lions of that region into "Bush" and "Plains" lions as if they were distinct races of that species. In a letter headed Congo Free State he acknowledges a copy of Selous's *African Nature Notes and Reminiscences*, which I had sent to him, and he writes that : "I was frightfully interested in it." He made a very large bag of elephants in the Congo, and made some money by selling the ivory. He was accompanied by a brother officer for a time who, I heard, got hurt by an elephant.

Then after other adventures he was appointed Governor of the Mongalla Province in the Sudan and wrote me from :

" (Kajokaji—Sudan, 11/7/1913.)

" Thank you for your letter of 1/4/13 and for your good wishes. I have had a letter from you on my table to answer for a long time. At last it got so long that another mail seemed to make no difference. I heard from your father, but his letter only arrived the day I left England, or it caught me in Paris, I forget which, but anyhow, it did not give me an opportunity of seeing him, which I should have done if it had come before.

" I have struck a good place here. I invented it and made it myself, and I am just hanging on till I get turned out. The Sudan, all I have seen of it, is pretty rotten. This place is 4,000 feet, and a sort of new Fort Manning which I have built myself. It is, to my mind, the best spot in the Sudan, so I am hoping not to be promoted, as wherever I am sent it could only be a rotten place.

" I have shot nothing for a long time except ' phunt ' and one can generally get 4 a year here, two on Sudan side and two in Uganda, and perhaps one or two out of Congo if one can get a licence.

" I have brought out a ·317 [he evidently means ·318, as there is no ·317 bore.—D.D.L.] this time, but lost the ammunition on the way. I have managed to borrow some to go on with, but have not done any ' phunting ' since I have been married.

" We have only been back here 6 weeks, and that time has been spent in settling down, rigging up furniture and getting all the back office work up to date. We are starting out on trek in a few days.

"I was so sorry I was so dilatory in answering your last letter. You seem to have done a good deal in the literary way lately ; I hope you make more money at it than I do. I put by all I make now, but I don't dare keep an account of stationery, ink, postage, etc., which, I think, would about swallow it up.

"We have got a little Duiker here which plays on the floor and stands on his hind legs to get ground nuts. His horns are just coming through and he sometimes practises butting at one's shins. My wife likes this place very much as there is a good garden and plenty to do.

(Signed) " C. H. STIGAND."

The only other letter I can find is written from :

" (Nimule, Sudan, 10/1/1914.)

"Thank you very much for your letter of 27/10/13, and for the copy of *Wild Life*, etc., for which I am very grateful. It was indeed nice of you to send it to me. People are apt to think that the gift of a book costs the author nothing, but I know that it is otherwise. It means either paying for it, or else forfeiting the esteem of some old aunt who would otherwise get a gift copy. I find that lots of people require free copies these days!

"I have just taken over Nimule as well as Kajo-kaji. It used to belong to Uganda, but is now ours since 1st January. It means extra work and keeping up two households, but does not seem to involve extra pay! We have just been trying to catch a young white rhino for the Cairo Zoo, but did not quite succeed although one got within a yard or two. They are beastly strong.

The only other excitement lately is that a leopard jumped in through the dining-room window after the dog, and died in the bathroom after making a fearful mess of our bedroom. They are very friendly at Kajokaji and come to drink milk in the kitchen! They take all the chickens, and got 15 out of my 17 ducks when I was on leave.

" Nimule is a more or less rotten place. I do not think that we will put in much time here, not more than we can help. All the old people in Africa thought it necessary to choose such unhealthy sites for stations. Such a lot of stations could be moved to good sites if the governments concerned would only realise that it is not absolutely necessary to occupy a site because Emin Pasha, or Baker or someone, was tired when he got there 40 years ago!

" Best luck, and hoping your new book will succeed.

(Signed) " C. H. STIGAND."

" PS.—I have lately made a frantic effort at producing a bread-winning book—*Hunting the Elephant.*

" C.H.S."

This book, *Hunting the Elephant in Africa,* was

published by Macmillan & Co. in 1913, and is a most interesting volume of shooting adventures. In it Stigand mentions the maulings he got from the rhino and the lion. The elephant accident occurred after it was published. Stigand was an untiring walker, and an excellent rifle shot. When I knew him in Nyasaland his favourite rifle was a Mannlicher ·256, and he preferred to use an aperture or peep sight. He took a great interest in snakes, and when he was stationed at Zomba he used to send a prisoner out on Zomba Mountain to bring him snakes. This prisoner was in for murder, and always had leg-irons on, but Stigand used to put him on parole and send him out alone, and though a murderer he was a man of honour, as he always came back with usually a deadly snake inside his only wrap, which was a brown army blanket, fastened to his body by a leather belt. Stigand would handle any snake he brought in, and one day a brown mamba spat in his eye and caused temporary blindness. This native had a wonderful knowledge of where to find these reptiles, and had some concoction rubbed into punctures in his wrists which he said acted as a preventive against being bitten. Stigand got him to prick his wrist, and was told that so long as he did not eat eggs he was safe from attack One morning he had asked me to breakfast with him, and his boy put down four eggs in front of each of us. He ate his, so I said : " What about snakes? " He then told me he did not believe a bit in the native's medicine, and only allowed himself to be inoculated to please the man, who treated the matter seriously.

He met his death in an Aliab rising on December 8th, 1919. These natives, a branch of the Dinka tribe, had risen in rebellion and committed murders, so troops were called in to settle the matter.

It was the time of the long grass, when it is difficult to get about a wild country, and Stigand was walking ahead of the troops with Major White, the C.O. of the Equatorial Battalion, when they were ambushed by a great number of the Aliab, who sprang up all round them in the thick cover. Stigand, White and a sergeant, Macalister, were killed, and when their bodies were afterwards recovered full of spear wounds, about a dozen of Stigand's fired cartridge-cases were found at the place where he had fought to the bitter end. Their bodies were buried near a spot called Kor Raby. Once, when we were talking about punitive expeditions against natives, I remember him remarking how easy it would be to fall into an ambush in thick bush or grass, and so it happened.

He was a wonderfully plucky fellow, and I am glad I knew him, and it will be a long time until his like is seen again in wilder Africa. He was a fine big-game hunter and a most observant field-naturalist, and as an administrator over primitive natives it would be difficult to find his equal.

In 1911, when I visited Nairobi in British East Africa (now called Kenya Colony), I met R. J. Cuninghame, who was at that time one of the best hunters in the country, as many of those who were lucky enough to obtain his services as a guide can acknowledge. There are men alive to-day who would be dead had it not been for his good shooting and coolness in danger.

He was born on July 4th, 1871, and died at Logan,

Wigtownshire, on May 23rd, 1925, and with his death there passed a man who, had he cared to do so, could have written one of the most stirring books on African adventure which has ever been penned, but he thought enough had been written, and was a modest fellow when it came to relating his personal experiences which were far greater than those of most people who have shot and travelled in wilder Africa.

On December 17th, 1889, he was awarded the medal and certificate of the Royal Humane Society for life-saving, and when the Great War broke out he was in German East Africa on a shooting expedition with Mr. R. L. Scott. They were reported as having been taken prisoners, but this was not a fact. Afterwards he served in France with an American ambulance, and then went to East Africa, where he became a political and intelligence officer, being awarded the M.C. and promoted major.

In 1924 I wrote and asked him some questions about the bags of lions made in Kenya, and received the following amusing epistle from him in reply, which runs :

" (Hensol, Mossdale, Kirkcudbrightshire, 5/12/24.)
" I have received your letter of the 1st of Decr. requesting me to supply you with detailed information regarding the number of lions killed by certain noted individuals. I have not the knowledge you require, and if I had, seeing that many of the men you mention are professional big-game hunters, it occurs to me that they would not be grateful to

myself if I quoted numbers against their names, which in all instances (seeing they have not retired) would certainly be under their actual total.

" If my memory serves me aright in 1911 Lord Delamere informed me that his bag up to then amounted to 52 lions, the bulk of which were killed in Somaliland. Since that date he may, or may not have secured further specimens.

" As regards the Percival brothers : A. B. Percival has been game-ranger and game-warden in the area recently known as B.E. Africa for a great number of years, and as he still is resident ex-officio in Nairobi, Kenya Colony, he can presumably obtain access to the official records of the game department. Leslie Tarlton, W. Judd, both the Hill brothers are still in Kenya Colony. Sir Alfred Pease is on his way, or has just arrived there. I suggest that seeing you require accurate data concerning the number of lions killed by all the above people that you address such member individually. The easiest way to make sure that your letters will be delivered is to address same to : c/o Safarilands, Ltd., Nairobi, Kenya Colony, E. Africa, together with a covering letter to the managing director of the above firm (of which Leslie Tarlton happens to be one) requesting that your letters be directed to the respective individuals. I am of opinion that Leslie Tarlton is far, in a way, the most skilled and successful hunter of Felis leo in all East Africa, and I am sure nothing would afford him greater pleasure than to do all in his power to collect the data you are in quest of.

"I do not think you have omitted any reputable East African sportsman or professional hunter, excepting, perhaps, an individual, by name Paul J. Rainey. This person was an American, and made a speciality of hunting lions with dogs imported from America. His methods did not appeal to the sporting instinct of the Briton, though he managed to account for a large number of lions in British East Africa. The individual himself is now defunct.

"I am of opinion that A. B. Percival would be able to provide you with a full description of his hunting methods, and the total number of lions he obtained if you appealed to him directly.

"As regards myself you are probably aware that after practising for nearly a quarter of a century I have retired from the trade. In my career I was chiefly engaged in the polishing-off of other people's partially incapacitated lions. Therefore it is quite impossible for me to hand you in any total. When not engaged on business I seldom disturbed the animal in question, on the same principle that a dentist does not occupy his holidays by endeavouring to extract Penultimate Molars.

"I have a full recollection of meeting you in Nairobi, and I think you were then accompanied by that splendid individual named Stigand—'Requiescat in pace.'

"Yes, I have read Bell's book. We all knew him as 'Karamojo Bell' and he was a remarkably fine natural rifle shot.

"As regards the writing of a book I am credibly

informed by Holy Writ that of the writing of books there is no end, and seeing that I have never made a beginning I consider I have reached the end.

"During recent times I consider that the book recently out by Dr. Christy is far on the way the best reading I have known for many years.

(Signed) " R. J. CUNINGHAME."

Towards the end of this volume I am enabled, through the kindness of Mrs. R. J. Cuninghame, to give me a copy of a most interesting lecture he gave, and also some notes which are sure to interest all hunters.

When in Fort Jameson, north-eastern Rhodesia, in 1903, I first met T. A. Barns, since known until his premature end as T. Alexander Barns. For a time, about 1905, we had cattle ranches of 3,000 acres each, with the boundaries adjoining, at a distance of about thirty-three miles from Fort Jameson, and situated near the old Tete road some 250 miles north of the Zambezi river. Neither of us stuck to farming long, as it did not seem to pay, owing to losses from disease and the inferiority of the grazing. Barns was an excellent walker, and through his powers of endurance was a successful elephant hunter. He was not a great rifle shot, but was cool, and therefore steady, and he believed after putting in the first shot, in pumping the whole contents of his magazine into the animal. When I knew him he mainly used a German-made 7·9 mm. Mauser, fitted with a hair trigger, which was a pull I personally disliked, although several men I knew liked hair triggers.

He wrote me about a trip he made to Lake Bangweolo, when he was successful in shooting many situtunga and other game. Here is the letter :

" (Fort Jameson, N.E. Rhodesia, 8/3/06.)

" I was very glad to receive your postcard, funnily enough I was wishing I knew your address just before I got it.

" I did fairly well on the Bangweolo Flats, bagged 11 Lechwe (1 black), 14 Sassaby, 13 Situtunga and some wonderful Puku.

" I'm getting up a great connection with skins and skulls, have one certain order for entire elephant and rhino skins. I received £150 for last elephant skin, not including value of tusks. The administration has just given me leave to shoot a bull Giraffe under the undertaking that I send the skull and headskin to an English museum—that's good, eh? I arrived back yesterday from my trip, having been 6½ months in north. Am now starting to pack and send off specimens, and then to Katamanda and B.C.A. for the year's elephant.

" By the way, what did you make on your four Loangwa elephant? Were they good ones?

" There is every chance I shall have a ' gent ' from England out here this year, through my *Field* advertisement. Everything the same as ever here. Timmler has at last gone home and did very well on his trip but no ' funts.'

" Diagrams as asked enclosed. Don't forget to write me and let me know where you are and what doing.

" Good luck, and the gods be with you.

(Signed) " T. A. BARNS."

Barns shot and preserved the specimen of the African bull elephant now in the Natural History Museum in South Kensington, and supplied other specimens. He went on many collecting trips for museums and was a good entomologist. On one of his trips he went to the extinct crater of Ngorongoro, over 100 square miles in area. He was an expert photographer. He wrote several most interesting books, among which were *The Wonderland of the Eastern Congo* and *Across the Great Craterland to the Congo*. He was killed in Chicago on March 4th, 1930, by a train when he stepped backwards to escape being run over by a motor car. I much regretted hearing of his death, for we had some happy times together in Northern Rhodesia. Once, when following a wounded elephant, in crossing a muddy stream, his leg was gripped by a small crocodile. He thrust his rifle into the water and fired it and the croc let go. I saw him about three weeks afterwards and we spent some time arguing about the size of the croc from the space between the teeth-marks in his leg. I remember I put it at about nine feet, but he was inclined to judge it (although he did not see it) at eleven feet at least. His rifle— the 7·9 mm. German Mauser—had a bulge in the barrel just where the bullet had met the water, and we both agreed that the metal must have been good material by the fact that it had not burst.

T. ALEXANDER BARNS WITH A BULL ELEPHANT SHOT IN NORTH-EASTERN RHODESIA

Hyenas in the night had eaten part of the trunk

Barns was only in his forty-ninth year when Fate overtook him in America, and I have often since wondered how strangely destiny works, for here was a man who had experienced many narrow escapes in wilder Africa who met his end in the midst of the throbbing noise and disgusting complication of what can only be called an effete civilization. His wife accompanied him on some of his trips into the wilds, and was probably the first white woman to visit such places.

It was also in 1903 that I first met a man with whom I had much in common, as he was very keen on shooting and natural history. This was Martin Ryan, a short, tough man, who was a good walker and runner, and a very cool hand with elephants. He had lived in Ceylon where he had gone in for running Sambur deer and other game with a pack of hounds, finishing the matter with a knife, a sport which had been started long ago by Samuel Baker (later Sir Samuel—the African explorer), and which has been recorded by him in *The Rifle and Hound in Ceylon*.

A man who can do this must have good legs and wind, so Ryan was well cut out for an elephant hunter, when he has not only sometimes got to run hard after them, but also be pretty nippy when one is inclined to turn nasty.

For a time Ryan worked on a cotton plantation at M'soro and later got charge of the Government cattle farm near Fort Jameson, but between times he did a lot of elephant hunting and was a steady rifle shot at game, which is a different matter to being a good target shot.

Then in 1913, or it may have been a bit earlier, he ran a mob of cattle down to Southern Rhodesia, a trek of some four hundred odd miles, and found that he had to keep them in quarantine for a considerable time. He sent me a letter from :

" (Shagari, Hartley District, S. Rhodesia, 3/5/1914.)
" Thanks for your last letter received a few days ago. I intended going back to Fort Jameson this month, but also my ivory, etc., didn't fetch so much as I thought they would so I am shooting here again.

" I have invested in a few donkeys and am going to leave elephant alone for a bit.

" I can quite imagine how you pine for the wilds and I'd like to be in your shoes for a couple of months just for a change.

" Strange to say a few days before I got your letter and your first sketch of the stern shot at elephant I killed three elephants, one of which I shot a few inches below the highest point of the back—a little to the right, the bullet travelling diagonally towards the left side. I missed the spine, but got the kidneys, and the elephant travelled 300 yards, leaving, literally, bucketsful of blood spoor. I had to take this shot as the wind was choppy, and I rather hurried matters, with the result that a cow with very small tusks came sailing down on me, and was within less than 20 yards before I spotted her. I raised my rifle, and either that, or the sight of my bushy beard stopped her, and as I didn't want wee tusks I slewed the rifle in a quarter circle and shot the cow as I have described above. The curious cow, of course, turned tail when I shot.

"I bagged two others as they ran by and both dropped in their tracks, one hit in the neck—the bullet going clean through. (I find this an excellent shot, close up to the head and through the ear. I have shot three elephants with this shot and all have collapsed immediately.)

"The other I hit in the shoulder, rather forward. I also caught a baby elephant which followed me like a dog after I had given it a hammering.

"I sent it to a farmer, but it lived but three weeks or a month. I was offered £30 down, and £25 if it lived for 6 months by the Pretoria Zoo, but Fellowes, the chap who was looking after it, and who was half-shares with me, instead of selling, waited until I got in to Shagari, with the result that we made nothing on it.

"These hip-bone shots should be good. I have not studied them, but the outer joints (I think it is 3 inch on each side of the root of the tail) show up and should also be good, though one would not often take such a shot. I have measurements of distances between the various socket bones on both fore and hind legs, also measurements and notes on other shots, but they are not with me. I'll look them up some day and send them on to you if you care for them. Have you noticed an elephant has a distinct separate cavity for the heart?

"I am out on the veld again, have been for six days, and have shot only two warthog; game isn't abundant here. I am moving further afield to-morrow to try for some hippo.

"What is your opinion of Ross's ·280 ? I have an idea you rather didn't like it in the *Field*. I should like to try one, though I must say that a bigger bore, in my opinion, if you can shoot really straight with it, is preferable to the small bores.

" I don't think I have lost a single buck (elephants barred) that I have hit with the ·375—40 grains cordite—and I can shoot pretty well with it. It has a short barrel and Mannlicher magazine. I got a very fine rhino with it about 26 ins. front horn, and 14 ins. back horn. I don't recollect if I told you of it.

" I took up night spoor at 8 a.m. and shot him at 5.30. p.m., doing only about 12 miles. When I heard him chewing in the long grass the boys chucked their loads and cleared. This, fortunately, brought him out to investigate, and he spotted me, and walked towards me snorting. He (his body) was then behind a bush, and I could see his head, and a bit of the top of shoulders. I got him a nice one at 20 paces between neck and shoulder which found the lungs, and another as he rushed off on the left shoulder. He is the finest rhino I have ever shot. Shall finish this scrawl some other day.

" Glad you heard from Barns. I suppose he is as hard up as most of us—poor chap. I have not met Barns since he has been back. Yes, I heard Lewis has S.S. [Sleeping sickness.—D.D.L.] I hope, if it's possible, he will get over it, he is a very straight fellow, and has his sister, I hear, out at Fort Jameson. McCullough, I see, is likely to recover. Wasn't it at Chinunda's that Lewis caught it? [Both these men died afterwards.—D.D.L.]

" I've had to wire up to Fort Jameson to Greer to sell some of my cattle (£100) to pay cattle hire, herding, etc. It will make a hole in the herd. I wish I had them here as they'll go for a song in the north.

" Have you met any Rhodesian friends since you have been home? I hope you will get a shooting party. I have a mind to advertise myself, to take anyone, anywhere, even into sleeping sickness places."

[Then he adds, as he has found his measurements]:

" I find I've the measurements with me but they are roughly taken and are probably not exact to an inch or two. Can't sketch so make allowances. [Then follow a rough drawing of a whole elephant and the top of an elephant's head with various notes.—D.D.L.] I hope you will be able to read this, and if you can I wonder if you will make out what I am writing about. It's awfully uncomfortable writing on one's blankets flat on stomach.

" I notice my elephant has an extraordinary short tail, but that makes it look cocky and adds to its appearance. Don't you think so, what? It has also got a squint heavenwards which makes it look piously dangerous ! "

Still later, 29/5/14 :

" Since writing I have shot an Elephant, 2 Sable, 1 Roan, and 2 Kudu, all with the ·416. This is quite a good bag for 20 days' shoot in these parts.

"I met a hunter, Botha by name, a fine good-looking Dutchman. He advised using a heavy bore during this time of year as growth is so great, and snap shots are the usual ones obtained. He says one has to shoot often through grass and bush, and you don't know where you are shooting, and thus often lose game by using a small bore. I think he should have added that you are also liable to run on to dangerous game in the grass, such as elephant, rhino and buffalo. For these reasons I have been using the ·416. I find it A1, and I can get a quicker and steadier aim with it than with the lighter ·375.

" The elephant was a lone tuskless bull. I ran upon it in the thick stuff and got charged when I saw what it was. I made frantic motions to my boys to come along. One boy ran forward with my small rifle, and when he saw it charging me he ran back faster than he came. This, I know not why, amuses me whenever I think of it. The other was a well-grown calf and had been alone for several months. After several lone half-hearted attempts to capture it I shot it for meat. Such a pity the boys would not help. With the help of one good nigger I could have collared it, and it would have lived as it was used to foraging for itself. Perhaps it is as well I shot it as it would have grown up a cute,

dangerous beast—most unsportsmanlike, I know.
By bye, Lyell.   Best of luck to you.
(Signed) " MARTIN RYAN."

" PS.—By the way, the heart cavity is the
cavity of the breast.   The heart lies, apparently, on
the breast-bone and is incased on both sides of it.   I
am writing of an elephant's heart."

Martin Ryan was, like myself, always very keen
on getting inside his game to find out exactly how
and where the vital organs were placed, and knowing
I was greatly interested in this subject, most of the
letters I got from him had something to say about
the matter.

The only other letter I shall give from him was
written from :

" (Shagari, Hartley Dist., S. Rhodesia, 16/2/14.)
" Our letters have again apparently crossed.
Thanks for your last from home where you men-
tioned being busy getting your new book published.

" I have shot twenty elephants (the slaughter of
the innocents) since my sojourn in S. Rhodesia, and
only one decent bull, but alas he had but one tusk
and that broken.   It's a damned shame to slaughter
like this, but I must try and get away for a change,
and I am, I fear, useless for a useful life, and it is no
use tackling anything else than hunting.   One gets
peace if nothing else ' far from the madding crowd,'
and it's a grand life in one's after youth, when

dreams of ambition and hopes of a home are done with, especially if you're a lover of nature and a connoisseur of the beautiful. I am havering, I fear ; anyway, what are your plans ? I wonder if you will come out again hunting. It would be better not to do so if you can manage to keep away as the life, in spite of its charms, has serious drawbacks.

"Bulls are awfully scarce here. I was on the spoor of three for two days, gaining on them nicely, when suddenly the spoor assumed this appearance [Then follow marks of running tracks which Ryan sketches.—D.D.L.], with little kicks at the toes, and you know what that means ! They had winded a bally M'swena honey hunter's hut and my two days' trouble was in vain.

"I returned to camp yesterday, where I am following the example of John the Baptist, living on biltong and wild honey. I have run out of stores, and can't spare a boy to go in to Shagari, 35 miles, as one of my four is sick, and another is only a kid of about ten years of age.

"Look here, Lyell, all that Barns and other hunters have told me about the vital spots of an elephant are all wrong. I've cut up and dug into so many elephants recently that I know. The heart, for instance, is very low down—18 inches from the bottom will reach it. Barns says the edge of the ear ! Why, you would almost miss the lungs with such a shot.

"The heart appears to lie in a receptacle all of its own, the lungs start over the heart, and go upwards

and backwards towards the tail end, and appear to
be attached to the spine. At the edge of the ear,
where it lies across the shoulder and rather forward,
is a socket joint. It's a ripping shot, but not for the
heart. You can also reach this socket joint when
an elephant is facing you near point of ear.

"The ·416 (Rigby) is great. I've shot several
elephants, running shots, with it, and they dropped
like shot rabbits—neck and lung shots.

"I don't like long-barrelled rifles, the sights seem
so far away, and they are more difficult to hold
straight. Again, I don't believe in working for a
shoulder shot, or a brain shot. I have lost elephants
by doing so, so I think one should shoot as you first
find the beast, there is always the spine right along
the back, and also for the rear shot, and so many
socket joints—you are apt to lose your beast wasting
time for a good shot. I refer more particularly to
elephant.

"I hope you don't think I'm dictatorial, or trying
to lay down the law on these matters, but such is
my experience, and I like to get other experienced
hunters' opinions on my views and discussing things.

"I am off to-morrow again on a flying trek with
two boys for two or three nights to try and pick up
spoor of either elephant or buffalo and shall finish
this on my return. Good luck and good night.

(Signed) " MARTIN RYAN."

Ryan wrote me other letters which I kept, but
those I have given are the most interesting. He is

perfectly right about the true position of the heart and lungs in an elephant. The former organ lies about a third up from where the bottom of the body comes, and I know of many fine elephants being lost by a hunter shooting too high. The edge of the ear, where it comes on the shoulder when flat, is much too high, though I have noticed the size of the ear varies in different elephants. Ryan is correct, too, in the placing of the lungs.

When the Great War broke out Martin Ryan came home and joined up, and later got a commission in the 25th Royal Fusiliers and fought in German East Africa. I had a letter from there dated August 15th, 1915.

" Your note to Gwendwr Road was sent on to me here. I lost your address and I felt so much at sea in England that I had a feeling that I was somebody else, and that Ryan was still hunting in the wilds of Rhodesia ! So you must forgive my silence.

" Yes, I joined the 1st King Edward's Horse, and was with them for four months, but as there seemed little hope of getting to the front, and as I was offered a commission in this lot (25th Service Battn. Royal Fusiliers) to come to East Africa, I jumped at the chance of getting out of England. We have been here about three or four months. I am now in command of the only troop of M.I. in our regiment. I did an interesting patrol the other day. I was away in G.E.A. for a fortnight and saw some good country and goodly sights— lakes and bird life, etc. It wasn't Lake Victoria.

Saw no Germans. On my way back I did a bit of shooting. Shot a rhino, galloped after it and shot it from horse-back whilst it was going. Also had a rough time with a herd of buffalo. Got into some very thick bush and had to shoot one of them.

" One of my men was hurt a bit, his stomach slightly ripped, another was tossed and two porters damaged a bit. It took me half an hour or more to get all the men out of the bush. What fools Englishmen straight from home are—on the veld. I'll tell you the whole story one day! On the whole we had a most enjoyable trip, and it was the first time I had felt really at home since leaving Rhodesia.

" Can't give you much news of war here. My M.I. and I were sniped at some time ago, two mules were shot, and a bullet drilled my rifle butt and touched up my horse, but no other damage done. The Germans got away, but have since been captured (5 Germans and 5 or 6 Askari, I think). Isn't this a damnable war out in France, and on the Continent I mean. We have an awfully easy time in comparison.

" Best of luck to you, and drop me a line sometimes. I hear nothing of things Rhodesian now, do you ?

(Signed) " MARTIN RYAN."

Poor Ryan's promised story will never be told me, because he fell in action on October 18th, 1917.

On that day he was ambushed with part of his regiment, and he and his brother were both killed in a very hard fight. I heard he behaved splendidly, which those who really knew him would expect, for he was a very gallant fellow.   In fact, one of the best.

CHAPTER III

Sir Alfred E. Pease, Bt., Lt.-Col. J. Stevenson-
Hamilton, Leslie J. Tarlton, A. Blayney Percival,
J. A. Hunter, A. L. Barnshaw and St. George Littledale.

IN 1924 I was trying to find out from African hunters
the number of lions shot by themselves, and to get
authenticated information regarding the total shot
by others, and have already given a letter I received
from the late Mr. R. J. Cuninghame on this subject.

I wrote to Sir Alfred Pease, as I knew of his great
experience in East and other parts of Africa. His
fine work, *The Book of the Lion*, is one of the best
accounts of his own and others' experiences with
these animals which has ever been published, so I
applied to him for any information he could give
me, and here is his interesting letter, which he has
kindly allowed me to publish:

" (Pinchinthorpe House, Guisbrough, Yorkshire,
    13/12/24.)
    " I have to thank you for your kind and interesting
letter received more than a week ago.
    " I am afraid I have read very few recent books
on sport and travel—the fact is I am now ' a stay at

home' man, and in these days I cannot afford to buy books and only read the reviews of them in the papers.

"The only two great elephant hunters I have known were Neumann and Selous, if I omit some of the old Boer and Africanders I used to meet in South Africa and on the Portuguese border.

"Neumann killed many of his elephants with the heart shot, at, of course, close range with a ·303, also at times with a ·303 in the forefoot for first shot, when an elephant becomes a practically immoveable target. Latterly he used a ·450 cordite rifle.

"I have killed alone, or in partnership, not a few lions with the ·256 (bluff-pointed or ratchet ball), and I was, as anyone with the amount of practice I had would be, a good and accurate big game shot with my own rifles, and I cannot ever remember having killed a lion dead with a single shot from a ·256, though I have done it several times with a 10 bore and a soft lead ball.

"It is impossible for me to give accurate numbers for the bags of those you name. I believe no one has killed so many lions *alone and on foot* as Major James Stevenson-Hamilton. A letter to him at the Army and Navy Club, Pall Mall, would I am sure get you the best information available. He is the only man I know who has kept careful records, and who can be depended on for accurate information. He is also the best authority on lions, and has had much more experience of them than I have. I have taken part in killing many lions, and have done more ' rounding-up,' for others and ' standing-by ' than shooting. I do not think I have killed by myself more than 14.

" The Hill's (two cousins) have killed very large numbers together, and in the company of others. I did a great deal of lion-hunting with them, and Harold Hill told me that he had killed 137 lions from my places Kilima, Theki, Kitanga, and his own Katelembo in B.E.A. in 7 years. It really, I think, means he had taken part in the killing of this number.

" Cuninghame is now living in Scotland, and he would give you as good an account of B.E.A. bags as anyone and without embroidery. His address is : Hensol, Mossdale, Kirkcudbrightshire, N.B.

" Galloping lions, given a good horse and experience, is the least dangerous way of killing lions, and is the least dangerous when you are by yourself and have no responsibility for others. I may be wrong about this as I believe danger is also reduced to a minimum when dogs are used, and most of the South African lion hunters used dogs. I believe Selous got many of his with this aid.

" I sold my place in 1912 in Kenya, and shall do no more big game work I expect as I am 67 years old. Still I had a ' good day ' and have seen what never can be seen again.

(Signed) " ALFRED E. PEASE."

" PS.—If you happen to see my book, *Memoir of Edmund Loder*, you may possibly find some information of interest. Published by John Murray.

"I believe Delamere killed 21 lions in Somaliland but not many after."

I followed Sir Alfred Pease's advice and wrote to Major (now Lt.-Col.) J. Stevenson-Hamilton about the bags of lions he had made and knew about, and received two very interesting letters, which he has kindly allowed me to print here.

Here is Lt.-Col. J. Stevenson-Hamilton's most interesting letter:

"(Kirkton, Carluke, N.B., 25/11/26.)

"Your letter returned from South Africa has followed me here.

"As regards lions I cannot tell you the exact number I have shot in the last 25 years, but fancy it is between 150 and 200, of which about 150 were either walked up on foot or driven out to me, the rest shot over waterholes or kills, or in other unsporting manner, which can hardly count in a bag, but were part of my job in the Transvaal.

"I have always hunted quite alone barring the usual native trackers, and for the past 14 years have used nothing but a military long ·303, lions being as you know easily killed beasts, and one has 10 shots.

"However, if you are in search of records you must not apply to me, as I fancy I am nowadays barely in the front rank, and so far as I know the man with the world's record for lions shot in a sporting manner is Mr. Leslie Simpson, an American, who after many years spent as a mining engineer in

Johannesburg, now makes lion hunting his hobby
His bags have been mainly in Kenya and Tanganyika,
and in the past 15 years or so he cannot have killed
much under 300 ; mostly hunted alone and on foot.

" He never writes or advertises, and I know him
only through slight personal acquaintance and
friends. A large number of people have shot over
100 lions, and I don't think any of my rangers in
the Transvaal Game Reserve of over 10 years'
service have shot less, and Wolhuter has probably
touched 150.

" We found an annual bag of from 150 to 200
lions just about kept pace with natural increase in
the game reserve.

(Signed) " J. STEVENSON-HAMILTON."

This account of Mr. Leslie Simpson's great bag
of lions shot in such a sporting way is very interesting,
but I fancy Col. Stevenson-Hamilton's bag is as
fine a record, for the lions in the Game Reserve of
South Africa are probably worse beasts to tackle
than those of Tanganyika, where they are less
accustomed to molestation. The number killed by
Wolhuter shows that he must have retained a fine
nerve, for in his book, *Animal Life in Africa*, Col.
Stevenson-Hamilton told the story of how he
was mauled by a lion, and very few men after such
an experience would care to tackle more lions.
Wolhuter killed the lion which gripped and dragged
him with a sheath-knife ; and Sir Alfred Pease, in
the book I mentioned of his, told the same story,
which is one of the most remarkable on record of

an escape from a lion. It is interesting to read that Col. Stevenson-Hamilton believes in a ·303 for lions, as many people with much less experience of lions than he has had think a big-bore rifle is essential. There is no rifle made in a large or small bore which can make a certainty of stopping a lion or any type of dangerous animal, though a large-bore bullet has an advantage in striking energy. However, in my opinion, I have always believed in a small bore, because it is light and more accurate, and one has become accustomed to its shooting through more use on the smaller game.

One of the greatest lion hunters in East Africa is Mr. Leslie J. Tarlton, and I remember having a long chat to him in his office in Nairobi in 1911 about rifles and shooting. I have several letters he sent me, and here is an interesting one, which I hope he will not mind my giving.

" (Safariland Ltd., Nairobi, 3/11/26.)

" Your letter of 30th Sept. duly reached me a day or two ago, and it rather looks as though a previous missive of mine has failed to reach you, because you ask me about the number of lions shot by myself and others, and I replied to this query some time ago.

" The fact is I do not know how many I have killed. As I think I mentioned in my previous letter, the frenzied efforts to top the bag of lions killed by one man has, I think, degenerated into a very spirited contest of lying. After 35 years of Africa, I expect I can tell as big a lie as the next fellow, but I do not care to enter the lists in this connection, and all I can say is that I have shot quite a lot, not nearly so many as numbers of other people, and a good many more than some.

" You must bear in mind that the old safari days have gone, never to return. Lions now are hunted in six-cylinder cars, and very often run down in the open veld, and killed from the driver's seat. The days when Pease, Cuninghame, Delamere, and so forth, galloped lions and shot them with a small bore are the only days that count in my estimation, and a man who has fairly hunted-down and killed 50 lions ' off his own bat ' that way was entitled to more respect than a modern game slaughterer who goes out in a fast car, kills a dozen lions before breakfast, and returns to camp saying : ' Out on this quiet life ! '

" On the much vexed question of small bores, do you not think it so greatly depends upon the skill and knowledge of anatomy possessed by the individual user as to what constitutes the best rifle ?

" Karamoja Bell, I believe, swears by the ·256. Personally I use a ·275 high velocity, but I also think a great deal of the American Springfield, which with a 220 grains bullet is, I rather fancy, the best all round small bore in the world.

" I think the tendency to go in for ' Magnums " is being overdone, because they sacrifice smashing power for velocity and low trajectory. I have killed one or two lions with my little ·275, with shots that I did not expect to do harm, but at the same time it seems to me that with these very light

pointed bullets one is always a trifle uncertain just
what they are going to do in the heavy muscles of
the larger mammals. Take for example the brain
shot at an elephant. I think if you got hold of Bell
he would probably tell you that the reason he is so
keen on the ·256 Mannlicher is that the solid bullet,
in addition to being very long and slender, is round
tipped instead of the sharp Spitzer tip.

"However, I am afraid my own shooting days
are done. Being rather badly crippled with rheuma-
tism, and just in the straight for fifty, I am only
too pleased to give place to younger men, and let
them murder what is left of the African game, with
the extra powerful rifles now in use, plus these
beastly motor cars.

(Signed) " LESLIE J. TARLTON."

Above is a most interesting letter from a very fine
sportsman. I think, though Bell used the ·256
often, his favourite rifle when hunting elephants
was a ·275 Rigby Mauser, with the old-type blunt
175-grains bullet.

Having sent Mr. Tarlton a book, I got the following letter from him, and in it he describes an incident
with elephant which is interesting.

" (Nairobi, 10/1/27.)

" Many thanks for your letter of 29th Novr.
and for your interesting book on the elephant,
which I have just finished.

" You and I seem to think much alike in the

matter of rifles, and particularly for elephant. I have always been a votary of the ordinary round-pointed solid.

" Your comments on elephants helping each other when wounded interest me much, because personally I have never been quite sure that they do really help. The only direct evidence of any value I can offer personally rather indicates the opposite. For what it is worth I vouch for the truth of the following :

" About 1908 I was sitting overnight with a friend, hoping for a tusker from a herd that used to water at the spring beneath the tree. This spring bubbled up from beneath a rock platform, which was level with the water, but beyond the small pool was heavy treacherous clay and mud.

" The elephant came and also rain and thunder, so that the moon was obscured and shooting out of the question—so we huddled under our waterproofs and waited till dawn. Of course the herd had gone, but imbedded to his belly, and within about five feet of this rocky platform, was a baby elephant which raised Cain when we approached. So I left immediately, under the impression that his mother might appear any moment from the surrounding forest, and not being anxious to witness the meeting. Accident took me past the spot 24 hours later. The baby was still there, but only his head and trunk were above the mud, and I gave the poor little chap a friendly bullet to end his misery. This is the only instance I know of elephants getting bogged also.

Possibly the herd took our wind, and stampeded, but I doubt it. I state the facts, and leave you to draw your own conclusions.

" The motor car has destroyed hunting as we know it, and especially with lion and other plains loving animals it is now largely a question of cash, as to how much one can kill in a given time. Quite recently my company looked after a man of many millions, over 70 years of age, a good fellow, but very wealthy. Bag 20 lions in three months. Yet another millionaire—bag 26 lions in six weeks. All quite honestly shot in the open in broad daylight, but such a record would be impossible without the cars.

" If I ever write a book I shall cut out the hunting and comment on the personalities of the visitors. And the sad thing of all is, that there is a regular leavening of genuine good sportsmen, who long for the real thing, but who find that modern methods have driven the game so far afield, that old time methods are no longer possible.

(Signed) " LESLIE J. TARLTON."

I have left out a few parts of Mr. Tarlton's letter, but it is apparent that many people who have gone to hunt in East Africa since motor cars were introduced cannot see how their unsportsmanlike methods are looked down on by the old hands. It is absolutely impossible to impress the true ethics of sport into some people, and this hunting of game in motor cars is a most cowardly proceeding, and one

which ought to be prohibited by law for the protection of the fauna. If the authorities were only
strong enough, they could make such a practice
impossible, as all they have to do is to legislate that
offenders, after proof, will have their cars and
weapons confiscated. This would soon stop the
disgraceful proceeding, as nobody with any sense
would risk the loss of a valuable car for the sake of
a few shots at game from it.

I also suggest that such confiscated cars could be
handed over to the Game Department, which might
aid them in running down others who practise
this nefarious kind of butchery.

In cases of this kind soft methods will never be
of any avail, but the difficulty is that the higher
authorities, not only in Africa but at home, often
fail to see the full importance of preserving the
game against such iniquitous and ruinous operations.
The fact is that very few of the authorities are true
sportsmen or naturalists, and they really do not
mind whether the game is killed off or not, so the
Game Department has to do the best it can with a
very limited staff for the immense territory it has
to supervise, and the present laws for the protection
of the fauna, which are not strong enough for the
present-day methods of the poachers and butchers.

It is difficult to understand the mentality of any
individual who can think it sport to follow up
and run down, by the power of an engine, animals
on open ground, where speed is the only thing that
can save them, and where they can be kept in sight
for miles.

In bush or forest harassed animals would, of
course, soon escape by turning aside in thick cover,
but on plains they have not a vestige of a chance

of escape, so they soon get winded and have to slow up. If it were possible to bring in such a law of confiscation of the car and weapon used, it would mean the preservation of many beautiful animals, which, as a matter of fact, are much more pleasing creatures than the unsporting scum who murder them in this gross fashion.

One of the best-known hunters in British East Africa is Mr. A. Blayney Percival, who has had a great and varied experience of the game of that country.

In 1924 he brought out *A Game-Ranger's Note-Book*, one of the best volumes on East African sport and natural history I have read. It is full of interesting notes and shooting adventures, and will always rank as a standard work on that country, as it is written by a man who knows what he is writing about.

He was among the authorities I wrote to about bags of lions and he replied in this interesting letter :

" (Mamandu, Magadi Junction, Kenya, 28/1/25.)
" Thanks for your letter and congratulations.
" The book has gone well, and the critics that I have most respect for—men like yourself—have been most kind. I agree with you that there are far too many books on Africa written by men at the end of a first safari—at any rate these men do not know Africa, its people and game as either you or I do. Possibly we did think so after our first trip, but experience has left me, and I have no doubt

yourself, doubtful of every darned thing applicable to game or native.

"Now to actual killing. I shot most of my lions, say forty, with ·256 (mistake in book says ·265).

"I do not remember exactly, but I feel sure that two thirds of the lions did not need a second bullet, if one did it usually meant several more. When hunting alone I seldom fired till I had a lion just how I wanted him, and I shot to put him out of business. Soft nosed bullets I gave up long ago except for small stuff or in heavy rifle.

"I have seen in all about one hundred and fifty lion killed, seven in a day, the best day I got four before the rest of the party came up. The Hills in one way or another accounted for probably over a hundred (they or their party), Delamere about fifty single-handed. My brother with his parties about two hundred. Delamere is the only one that counts single-handed lions—all others count number of deaths they were in at. Rainey killed about 150 with his dogs, fine or poor sport as the case might be, the kill was the least part of it all. As he almost always put in the bullet I think that he probably killed more than anyone else to his own gun. Bags of twenty for a trip have been made more than once. I have been forgetting Leslie Simpson. His lone-handed bag is over a hundred, but he is such a retiring bird that one is apt to forget him. I give him the palm without a doubt. Rainey may have shot more in numbers, but with dogs and men to help, but Leslie Simpson has mostly shot alone. He got 26 in six weeks one time, and I do not think he shot one until he was fifty.

"If a man is prepared to pay for it, and doesn't mind how he gets a beast, it is now possible to kill any number of lions, say guaranteed bag of 25 for a couple of months, and so safe that a child or woman could do it. By the way a man took his nine year old son out the other day, within sight of where I write, and the boy bagged a lion, and the father got so excited at the fact he bagged himself in the leg, bullet came out the other side and did no damage, but he doesn't like it referred to!

"To get back to Karamoja. He has probably killed a thousand elephants, and all with small rifles. Twenty-five years ago when I first met him he was shooting with a ·303, and his judgment not many years ago was that the ·256 was the best rifle ever made from an all round point of view.

"Drop me a line when you strike any interesting facts or fables re game. As you know I am very keen on photography and will be glad to hear of anyone coming out here to take pictures of game.

"Best of luck. (Forgive mistakes of this machine.)
(Signed) " A. BLAYNEY PERCIVAL."

There has always been, and probably always will be, doubt as to who has killed the greatest numbers of

African animals such as elephant, lion and buffalo. We need not include the rhino, as, though he can be a dangerous beast at times, he is a blundering, excitable beast and fairly easy to turn or kill with modern rifles. Regarding elephants, which I do not consider as dangerous as lions, though they can be nasty enough at times, there are three men who top the list for numbers, and they are : W. D. M. Bell, Arthur H. Neumann and James Sutherland. Others who have shot a great number are Anderson, Banks, Boyes, Blunt, Buckley, Barns, Pearson, Sir A. Sharpe, Brittlebank brothers, Salmon, Black, Tarlton, Cuninghame, Selous, Stigand, Ryan and a Greek and an Italian I heard of. The most expert shot of the lot was probably Bell, and I have heard him described as a " wizard " with a small bore rifle.

The records for lions probably belong to Stevenson-Hamilton, Leslie Simpson, Leslie Tarlton, the Percivals, J. P. Lucy, Lord Delamere, Clifford and Harold Hill, Cuninghame, Rainey, Hunter and Dan Mahoney. Selous only shot thirty-one, and there are many men whom I have not mentioned who killed far more lions than Selous. It does not follow, however, that the man who has shot great numbers of a certain animal knows more about its habits than someone else who has killed a mode-rate number, for when one man is simply concen-trating on killing another may spend more time and thought on observations !

About buffaloes—Selous killed over 200, and long ago, in Portuguese East, men like Cuninghame, Mahoney, Pooley, Larsen and others, who shot them for their hides, slew enormous numbers in that great buffalo country. Most of these were shot with old ·450 Martini-Henry rifles, I believe, for these rifles were sold cheap and ammunition was easy to procure in the country. It is a pity to think that money enters so largely into the question, for had elephants no ivory, lions no fine skins, and buffaloes no good heads, meat and hides, they would all have been more immune from persecution at the hands of ruthless man.

To hunt for a good trophy, or for the thrill of the thing, is one thing, but to slaughter for "filthy lucre" is quite another. There are some good sportsmen left, but mighty few; and the modern magazine rifle, though a fine weapon when moderately used, becomes a curse in the hands of an excitable sadist who uses it like a machine-gun. The expert may use a magazine because he likes to feel he has a few spare shots "up his sleeve," but he takes as much care with his first (the important) shot as possible and picks his spot. It would really be most sporting to use a single-loader ·256 falling-block, so as to give the game a chance, and feel that one is "playing the game," but few single-loaders are as reliable as magazines, and some of them have a habit of jamming badly!

When game cause destruction to plantations or the natives' fields the Government is expected to keep them in order and reduce their numbers, so in places like Uganda the game-rangers do the necessary thinning out.

About 1927 lions were doing damage to natives and live stock in the Masai Reserve, so Mr. J. A. Hunter was sent to teach them a lesson, which he effectually did, as he killed ninety-eight, and probably some wounded ones died. He wrote me this letter about some of his experiences:

" (Nairobi, Kenya, 23/3/28.)

" Many thanks for your enquiry re lions in the Masai district to which I would have replied earlier only I just returned from hunting with the Rothschilds' safari yesterday.

" It may interest you to know that on this recent month's safari in Kenya, near the Tanganyika border, we saw in all forty-three lions in the open, securing twelve of them. One is now restricted to four lions under a licence.

" It seems hard to believe, even in these days, that there are yet several unhunted places where big game is most certainly on the increase.

" The Baroness Rothschild is probably one of the finest rifle shots I have yet seen, and used exclusively a ·256 Mannlicher (short barrel).

" On my recent trip for the Government I could write much, and I had certainly to hunt for all I knew to secure these marauding beasts. Was most disappointed to find the great game reserve in the Southern Area was more or less derelict of game. I refer specially to the smaller fauna, and hunger caused by the scarcity of game undoubtedly made the lions the scavengers I found them. Hyænas were swarming, and it was no uncommon sight to see troops of these badly made beasts chasing a lone zebra or Kongoni in broad daylight.

" I used a light model magazine ·416 Rigby— short barrel—and could not wish for a rifle with better stopping power, and as I was entirely alone could not afford to take undue risks. In two places on the Selengei sand river, about twenty miles west of Sultan Hamud station, rhino were so numerous that they hampered my hunting. I became very expert in continually dodging them, but had to stop one very big bull at close range. Have used practically every make and calibre of rifles, and have good faith in the ·256, ·275, ·280 Ross (in a Mauser action), ·318 and ·300 Springfield cartridge. The latter I was loath to try, being American, but the genuine Mauser with 24 in. barrel taking the ·300 cartridge and 180 grains bullet is a most perfect small bore weapon with great stopping power.

"I have the material and data on all species of big game which I dare say would make a useful, interesting and educational book, etc.

(Signed) "J. A. HUNTER."

Having sent a reply to this interesting letter advising him to give others the benefit of his great experiences in a book, I got the following letter :

" (Nairobi, Kenya, 8/6/28.)
" Very many thanks for your letters and offer of assistance to help me. [This refers to trying to find a publisher for him, I think.—D.D.L.] I appreciate it very much and am guided by what you mention. Would have written earlier, but only returned from a safari a few days ago.

" On this last trip we saw thirty-one lions (mostly in twos and threes) ; and shot five nice-maned specimens. Lionesses were in the majority, but my client, a good sportsman, vied with me in ' sparing the hens.' One afternoon we came on six males together (three of them very big lions) ; but not one of them with a mane, and after taking a photo carried on. It is strange that even in these days of civilization you can go out from my hunting grounds, and practically every day see lions sitting about near dongas, and apparently quite at ease. This is down in the fly area and apart from a few Wandorobo no natives to molest them as the Masai will not take their stock there. I would mention that these fly are non-dangerous to human beings. . . . The snake was the black mamba [Referring to a photograph sent to me.—D.D.L.], and rises about 18 in. from the ground—very fast and a real nasty customer. Have killed lots of these from time to time, although Kenya is wonderfully free from snakes, and often I go a month without even seeing one. A few months ago, having shot a similar snake, after a few minutes I noticed something protruding from its mouth, and on investigation, and pulling it out found it to be another mamba (same species and 5 ft. long). This shows that these reptiles actually eat one another. I wonder if you have come across a similar incident ? I skinned both snakes, and this meal can only have been made an hour or so previous.

" I am going out again about the 18th July after elephant, rhino, buffalo and lion chiefly, and expect to return here about the 20th September, so will be pleased to hear from you again at any time.

" An elephant hunter called Goss from Tanganyika is at present staying with me, and on looking through his negatives I noticed one of a python killing an Impalla. I am having a few prints given to me from it, and will send you one in the course of a day or two.

" With renewed thanks and trusting you are well.

(Signed) " J. A. HUNTER."

In 1903, when in Nyasaland, I met a man named A. L. Barnshaw, who at that time was the agent for the British Central Africa Co. at Gwazas, on the Upper Shire River. He soon left for the north to hunt elephants and was fairly successful in shooting some good bulls. While stopping with him I noticed hanging on the wall of his bungalow a very fine bushbuck skull and horns, so I asked him where he shot it, and he told me it was a head which had been picked up in the bush, and that the animal had probably been killed by a leopard. Having asked him if I could measure it, I got out my steel tape and took several measurements and made the horns 19¾ inches on the curve. I told him this was the record at that time and advised him, if he wished to sell it, to write Rowland Ward. Afterwards he wrote me that Ward had given him £12 for it, as well as a copy of his book on " Records." This head remained the record for some years while in the hands of Lord Rothschild, but in the 8th edition (1922) *Records of Big Game*, comes only sixth. The best head in this year is one of 21¾ inches on the curve. Nyasaland is a good country for bushbuck, which is an animal well distributed throughout Africa.

After Barnshaw had done some hunting he wrote me a letter from which I extract interesting notes on elephant. He writes :

" (Kasama, N.E. Rhodesia, 6/4/07.)

" Yours of 23/1/07 reached me yesterday in the veld as my mail has been following me about for nearly a week, I having started from camp last Saturday on elephant spoor and am only just back to-day.

" I got up to a herd of 10 to 12 large bulls, and about 40 to 50 cows and calves, but at the critical moment was put off by a cow and so only got a snap shot at the bull I wanted—a 70 to 80 pounder. I wounded him, but he got away and I eventually lost him.

" I am trying to get my third (elephant) for this year now having shot two 30 pounders ; and afterwards I'm off to German E. Africa to try there again. So far I have bagged 12 bulls ranging from 80 and 74 lbs., 67 and 45, 54 and 54, 40 and 38, 70 and 48½, 32 and 31, down to 15 lbs. each. I forget all the weights but these are my biggest.

" Rhino and other game I don't trouble my head about unless I fall across them. I have bagged several rhino, hippo and a quantity of other game down to Thomson's gazelle and Topi, only found in G.E.A. Also plenty of Situtunga and Black Lechwe. In fact there are lots of Lechwe here. I have also had one or two turns-up with Buffalo which seem especially vicious round here. One of my best fundis (tracker) has been crippled by a buffalo cow.

"I had a bad experience with an elephant in January. I got up to him and was looking at him from about 15 yards off, not meaning to shoot as I thought he was too small (35 and 31 lbs.) when he came for me bald-headed. I was behind a small 8 inch tree, and in his rush he scraped some of the bark off. Luckily I stood and waited till he got level with me, and then let rip at his heart, my rifle barrel almost touching him. However, he went about four miles and tried to be wicked when I went up to finish him. He had five fresh Kaffir wounds in him, and no doubt that made him savage. But strange to say his lungs were one mass of froth, and my bullet made a hole you could put your fist through in his heart, and then he went at least four miles and was ratty at the end.

"Three of us up here have had bad times with nasty elephants this year, in fact I've nearly been blotted-out on four occasions lately—that is this year. Norton had an elephant throw a large piece of tree at him, and then charge, and Cookson nearly got scuppered by a cow, in fact all the Boma men up here have shot cows and got off. Norton, Creed and I are the only ones who haven't killed females.

BULL ELEPHANT SHOT AND PHOTOGRAPHED BY GEORGE GARDEN

AN EXPERT HUNTER AND GAME PHOTOGRAPHER

" Well, I think that is all the news, you always ask me to write long letters, but you don't send more than forty words yourself, is paper scarce with you or ink ?   Well, good luck, and do not kill any more 'lady' elephants—it's not sportsmanlike !

(Signed) " A. L. BARNSHAW."

In above letter Barnshaw describes how an elephant ran a long way with a bullet-hole in the heart, but he does not say whether it was at the top or the bottom of that organ.   A wound in the upper part usually brings an elephant down within fifty yards or so, because the big arteries are cut, which soon causes death.   A puncture in the bottom, however, is not nearly so instantaneous in results, and the wounded animal may run some way, so I am sure Barnshaw's example had a lower heart wound.

Several times I have mentioned in my writings the result of different shots, and although this is not a nice subject it plays such a part in humane killing that I shall write again about it.

The heart is about a third up from where the chest runs between the forelegs, and dead broadside on requires the bullet to hit the flat of the nearer foreleg.   Therefore, when taking this shot the best position is to get a little behind.   This organ is huge and I regret I never measured and weighed one, but from memory and the size of a cushion near where I write which appears about the same length, I got out my tape and find it is 18 inches.   This, of course, is for a bull.

On getting a shot in the heart, an elephant, if one

is close enough to see it, may give a shiver. He will then dash off, sometimes grunting. If a bullet goes near this organ, or by mischance hits his stomach, this has usually an exasperating effect, and such an animal will likely be very nasty, which is natural as one cannot expect animals not to resent their injuries at times.

The lung shot is not very satisfactory with modern small bores, though a wound even from a ·256 through both lungs will kill, but the animal will likely run a long way. Such an injury often produces a strange result, as the beast, after going hard for distances up to a mile, will slow up, then stop and throw his trunk straight up in the air several times. This is akin to the towering partridge, which goes upward to get air, as it chokes through a suffusion of blood in the lungs and respiratory organs.

Most of the small-bore exponents prefer the brain shot, which, if correct, causes instant death, and from broadside this is from 4 to 6 inches forward of the ear orifice. The better plan is to shoot from slightly behind and put the bullet into the orifice itself.

An elephant which drops to the brain shot does not move, except, of course, there will be spasms for a space, due to muscular contraction caused by nerve paralysis. In a book which I was recently asked to contribute to I made the remark when writing on this point that : " Should an elephant, after falling, make the slightest movement, it is best to run in from behind and put one or two bullets into his ear-hole, ranging forward, etc." Here I forgot to mention this muscular contraction which one does not always have the chance of seeing on account of bush or grass.

The ·256 or ·275 old-type cartridges with blunt-point solids had wonderful drive, and even the ·303 was good with a solid as I have seen one go slick through the upper part of a big bull elephant's skull, and do the same in a rhino's body, which is pretty thick just behind the shoulder.

Do not use pointed solids, as, if the point gets bent on a round bone, they are easily deflected. If not turned aside they have marvellous penetration.

Heart blood is the ordinary colour, lung blood light coloured and frothy, and kidney blood the colour of stout (dark brown).

My old friend Ryan took a great interest in vital shots, and the position of the vital organs in elephant, and like myself did (with native help, of course) a good many post-mortems on their carcasses. This is the only way of getting real knowledge of where to place the shots. Many fine elephants have been lost through people shooting too high for the heart with the idea that it is a third down from the top instead of a third up from the bottom.

In a letter dated May 29th, 1907, Barnshaw writes me about getting three elephants with tusks weighing from 30 to 52 lbs., and he said that he had lost eight big bulls, one having 84 and 86 lb. tusks, which, after he had given it up, was followed and shot by a hunter named Norton. He also says : " I am sending you the skin of a stoat or weasel, the Awemba call them Kampandwe. They seem to live on rats, mice, etc., and are nocturnal and fairly well distributed all over the country. They live in holes in anthills and old trees and are very rarely seen. Unfortunately I could not get the head, but in appearance it is very like a stoat or ferret. I've never seen one before, and the boys say they are very hard to find and catch. This one was after some eggs when killed." In a postscript he adds : " I shot a strange animal this year. It was a bushpig with warts like a warthog, but quite distinct as you know the warthog's four. Have you ever seen one like that ? " I wonder if this was a warthog—bushpig hybrid ?

The small ferret-like animal was an animal of the stoat or weasel species, and it is called by the Chinyanja "Likongwe," by the Yaos " Chindindi," by the Chikunda "Likongwe," and by the Angoni "Ndendi," or "Chakida." The Awemba, besides calling it "Kampandwe" also use the word "Koti" for it.

In tropical Africa there must be many small animals still unknown to science. Many of these, being nocturnal in their habits, are seldom seen and caught, and the Likongwe is one of them.

Writing to me again from "The Veld," via Songea, in German East Africa, Barnshaw, on 30/9/07, writes of getting a good bull with tusks of 70 and 50 lbs.—the smaller having apparently been broken, judging from the difference in weight. He now says that the reason he lost so many bulls was that he found his cartridges were bad, because they had been removed from the zinc boxes for some time. Having opened up a fresh lot, he says they are all right. The damp in the rains should not affect cartridges even when removed from an airtight case, and if one keeps them fairly dry, they will be good for several seasons. I found Government ·303 ammunition was good, and German D.M. 7 mm. (·275), 7·9 mm. and 9 mm. cartridges were excellent, and I never had a misfire. On the other hand, I have had 6·5 mm. (·256) of the rimless type

very bad, as the ends of the cases split, and sometimes
left the bullet in the chamber and spilt the powder
there and in the magazine when a cartridge was
ejected.

I never thought the ·256 Mannlicher-Schonauer
rimless cartridge quite so powerful as the old-type
rim ·256 cartridge, and this idea was corroborated
in a letter I got from Mr. St. George Littledale,
written from Wick Hill House, Berks, on September
22nd, 1926.   He writes :

" In 1895 Sir Edmund Loder gave me a Mannlicher
rifle, bayonet and all complete, on the eve of starting
for Tibet.   Had only time to have sighting altered.
On my protesting that I had a room full of rifles
and did not want any more, all he said was try the
Mannlicher, and like Lily Langtry and the famous
soap I have used no other since.

" In my opinion the original Mannlicher was
more deadly by far than either the Schonauer or the
Magnum.   Speaking from memory, and it is a
long time ago, I got the first 40 or 50 animals I
fired at without requiring a second bullet at any of
them.

" With the Magnum I fired at a stag at about
200 yds., it never moved and the stalker said : ' You
are over his shoulder.'   He did not move so I
fired again with some irritation.   The stalker said :
' You are over him again.'   So again I fired with
undisguised disgust.   He said : ' Over again,' so I
brought the rifle down and looked at the sights,
making sure they must have been shifted.   While

looking at them the stalker said: 'He's down.'
A half crown would have covered the three bullet
holes, and what the gillie saw were the bullets
striking after they had gone through the heart.
The Magnum is a wonderfully accurate weapon
and I consider it adds a couple of hundred yards to
the distance at which beasts can be shot, but is that
an advantage, very questionable.

"In the old days of ' Express ' rifles the cream of
the sport was the crawl from 200 yds to one hundred.
That is all over now, and so I am afraid is my big
game shikar.

(Signed) " ST. GEORGE LITTLEDALE.

"Am glad I made a good shot (quite a Magnum
Mannlicher affair) in selecting your name from the
Shikar Club list."

The " PS." refers to having mislaid my letter,
and then found my name in the list mentioned.
The writer's reference to Lily Langtry and the soap
is new to me, as I thought " Since then I have used
no other " referred to a tramp picture by Harry
Furniss.

Mr. St. George Littledale was a most remarkable
shot, not only at game, but in making groups at a
target. He was one of the first Englishmen to shoot
in the Pamir, and wrote an interesting account
of his trips in The Badminton Library, Vol. II. He
brought home many splendid heads of Ovispoli
and other game, and mentions using a ·500 Henry
" Express."

Apparently, like others, when he tried the little .256 Mannlicher he found it so superior that he stuck to it, as its accuracy, killing power and lightness are wonderful. The small weight of the ammunition as compared to bigger bores is a great advantage on long hunting trips.

Another well-known sportsman who shot a lot in the Himalayas was Major C. S. Cumberland, and he also used a ·500 Henry rifle in early days. He wrote a book called *Sport in the Pamir and Turkistan Steppes*, which is well worth reading. On one of his trips I believe he got a bad festering toe on one foot, probably through a blister, and the story goes that he cut the toe off himself, as he was far from a doctor, and did not wish to return before he had got the trophies he wanted.

Major Cumberland came to Nyasaland on a shooting trip about 1911–12, for a friend told me that he had been enquiring as to where I was to be found. Unfortunately I was away on a hunting trip at the time, and by the time I returned to my main camp he had gone back to England, so I missed seeing a man I would have much liked to meet.

When I was a youngster I lived with my people at Monifieth, about six miles from Dundee, close to the estuary of the Tay, where I got a fair lot of wildfowl shooting. This was one of the haunts of John G. Millais when he was taking an interest in the birds of the coasts, for as a youth he used to roam round Scotland collecting birds.

One of my chief delights, as I began to take an interest in sport and natural history, was to visit the whalers when they returned to Dundee from their northern cruises after whales and seals.

One of the best known of the whaling skippers was Capt. Adams, who commanded first the *Arctic* and afterwards the *Maud*, in which ship he had, I believe, an interest. Some of the names of these old whalers were a romance. Take, for instance, the names *Aurora*, *Thetis*, *Polar Star* (or was it *Polaris ?*), *Esquimaux* and *Chieftain*, with their iron-sheathed stems, and their figure-heads. The *Thetis*, I remember, had a finely carved woman, and the *Chieftain* a Highlander. Then the officers and crews were a very fine lot; not saints, perhaps, but men of a stamp we do not see amongst seamen to-day. My favourite friend was a great tough-looking harpooner in the *Maud*, who, I think, had followed his skipper, Adams, from the *Arctic*.

His height was full six feet, and he was very powerfully built, and had a long tawny beard —a regular Viking if ever there was one. He used to take me below and show me the rifles, and the lances for giving the *coup de grâce* to the whale fighting for its life and freedom. The sealing rifles were mostly single bottom-lever falling-blocks ·450 "Express" by Alexander Henry, of Edinburgh, with a side lock and a big hammer, and I remember noticing that some of them had the lock placed to the left and not the right. These rifles were regulated for a 270-grain bullet, with a copper plug in the hollow point, and I used to think these plugs were caps to act explosively, until I found that they were simply plugs to cover the hole. These weapons so fascinated me when I thought of the Polar bears, walrus, musk-ox and seals they had slain that when I went to India my father gave me one—the first shot at a starling on a chimney-pot blowing the starling and a good bit of the apex to smithereens, much to my dad's disgust when he heard of it.

The Capt. Adams mentioned was perhaps the most prominent of the Dundee whaler skippers. He had helped the Government with information in connection with exploration, and was greatly experienced in Arctic conditions.

My father offered me a trip to the Arctic regions, and it was almost settled when a message came that the small cabin was needed for two Government men who had to go north. We had been told there was a possibility of the cabin being reserved for them if they were going, but it was thought that they would choose another ship. When I was told I could not go I think it was one of the greatest disappointments of my early life, for I had looked forward to getting a shot at something big, such as a bear or a caribou.

Capt. Adams brought home an Eskimo named Oomiak on one trip, and he had brought his kayak (canoe), and a friend and I took the man to a big pond, where we tried it. They are cranky craft, and it needs long practice to work them by balance and the use of the double paddle. On my first attempt I got an upset, but only wet one arm up to the shoulder, as the water was shallow at the side of the pond. Oomiak was, like most of his race, a small, stocky man, with jet-black hair and features like a Mongolian. Before he returned to the Arctic regions he was presented with all kinds of things, such as knives, needles, pipes, tobacco and beads, etc., and would be a rich man when he returned to his friends.

When I am writing of the whalers I must mention the incident of the Tay whale which I saw being chased. This whale had come up the Tay from the sea, and three boats were sent from the whaling vessels in Dundee harbour. Two of the boats got "fast" and were pulled by the whale up the coast, but when night came on they had not been able to finish it with the lances, though it had been badly wounded, so they had to cut the lines and return to port. Two days after, however, the whale died and was washed ashore, I think, near Peterhead. An old man in Dundee named Johnnie Woods bought the carcass and got it to Dundee. I think it was towed south by a tug. Anyhow, he had got it ashore near a part called the Stannergate, and I went to see it. By this time it had gone "high"; in fact so odorous that the authorities requested its removal, so it was boiled down, and the skeleton is now in the Dundee Museum.

Once when on the deck of a whaler, all slimy with blubber which was being unloaded, I slipped and slid along, and my Harris tweed knickerbockers were so smelly that they had to be sent to the cleaners.

I was reminded of Johnnie Woods's whale, and my pants, when I brought some hippo hide down the Zambezi in a boat. The skin got wet and the great heat made it smell most offensively. When I got to Chinde I was requested by the Portuguese commandant to order its removal, so it was sent a mile up-river and deposited on a sandbank, where, I suppose, the hyænas on shore and the crocodiles in the river enjoyed an unexpected feast. The smell on my khaki pants reminded me of the blubber on the whaler, as everything that had touched the rotting hide was extremely niffy. Some elephants' tusks, wrapped in sacking, were tainted so strongly that the European assistant who superintended the storing of them was nearly sick, so I asked him how he would have liked, as I had done, to sleep close to a much stronger smell for quite two weeks, as my bed was made on the platform at the stern every night, where the aroma was at times so pungent that it almost made me ill.

When I am writing of smells I have not forgotten a camp I made close to a dead elephant, the flesh of which had been piled in a big heap just outside my tent. I had sent to the Angoni villages round my permanent hunting camp on the Bua river, some thirty miles away, to tell them to come for the meat, but they had delayed. By the time some fifty women came the meat had lain in the sun for four days, and the flies were buzzing round it in a cloud and laying their eggs in it. The wind changed one day and instead of my tent being up-wind it had now got on the lee side. This happened after I had turned in, so my men were surprised to be turned out about 10 p.m. to re-pitch my tent to windward. No sooner had this been done than the breeze went back to its original quarter, and I almost got asphyxiated in the stench. I smoked most of the night as I did not wish to trouble my boys and carriers again, and had a bad headache next morning which was probably a combination of gas and tobacco.

When in France during the war I often, like others, got many whiffs of gas, but if the results were deadlier than dead elephant, they were certainly less unpleasant to breathe.

CHAPTER IV

Brig.-Gen. Sir R. Pigot, Bt., D.S.O., M.C., and John G. Millais.

WHEN I was in Africa I had several rifles by Daniel Fraser of Edinburgh, who is now dead, and his firm out of business. His rifles were the most beautifully sighted weapons I ever saw, and he took great pains in the finish of his rifles. A little single ·303 I had by him was very nicely balanced, but the side lever was not very satisfactory, as after the chamber got slightly corroded by using inferior ammunition it used to jam and nearly got me into trouble on several occasions. Sometimes, when I could not open the lever with my right thumb, I put the stock on the ground, and forced the breech open by pressing it with the flat of my boot, but such treatment on an otherwise perfect rifle always seemed to me atrocious, except that it was the only thing to do so as to get the fired case from the chamber of the rifle.

Another good Fraser rifle was one of the early ·318 bores, but here again I had bad luck, as the ammunition I had brought out with it was defective. Often three rounds out of five would misfire, so this also was often a danger. There is nothing that puts a man off his shooting more than misfiring cartridges, as it not only spoils one's shooting, but brings an uncertainty as to what will happen next when one is at close quarters with dangerous game.

After reading a most interesting book entitled *Twenty-five Years' Big Game Hunting*, by Brig.-Gen. R. Pigot, D.S.O., M.C., I wrote the author about rifles, as he gave an interesting chapter about them, in which his opinions ran on much the same lines as my own, and got the following letter on the subject :

" (Brickworth House, Whiteparish, Salisbury,
    17/2/30.)

" Thank you for your letter, of course I know you well by name.

" I think even the military experts now consider the Lee-Enfield action a bad one compared to the Mauser, and I have always understood that the new Service rifle which they intended bringing out just before the war (I think) had a Mauser action. Now we shall no doubt have to wait a long time before they change it since war and therefore rifles are out of date ! So they tell us. I wonder whether you agreed with my remarks about the peep sight. It was Fraser who first induced me to use this, and I have never used anything else since, but I have met very few men who will use it even when they have it on their rifle.

" The last rifle I had from Fraser was a ·360/·320 magazine, the best rifle I have ever used. I am still using it with the 1913 cartridges. At present these cartridges show no sign of deterioration, though I have had them backwards and forwards in hot and cold countries. I am wondering, however, how much longer they will last.

"Another point as regards Fraser rifles will perhaps interest you. I have a Fraser ·360 falling-block action. When Fraser was still doing business I had no difficulty with the cartridges which I got from him. Now out of every packet of 10 that I buy, some 2 or 3 only are a proper fit. A pair of callipers, and in some bad cases even the naked eye, show a very considerable difference in the thickness of the rim.

"I maintain that Fraser made his rifles so accurately that only a perfectly fitting cartridge would go in and allow the action to close. This ·360 cartridge is now out of date, I know, and therefore turned out in a slipshod manner by the cartridge maker combines, and probably good enough for any ·360 rifle which is not a Fraser. I feel quite sure that Fraser himself would never have accepted them.

"I hope if ever you are in these parts that you will come over to lunch or for the night.

(Signed) " R. Pigot."

This is the kind of letter about rifles I like getting as it deals with the finer points of the subject. Many people who use rifles forget the quality of the ammunition they buy. Doubtless on the

whole British manufacturers are probably ahead
of foreigners in the quality and dependability of
their cartridges, though there are exceptions. I
think, on a previous page, I mentioned how good
the German " D.M." ammunition was for 7 mm.
and 7·9 mm. rifles, and they were the most reliable
cartridges I ever saw made for Mauser rifles. The
6·5 mm. for the old-type Mannlicher was also
excellent, and although I fired quite a number of
all these three types I cannot remember having
a misfire with any of them. The 6·5 mm. cartridge
for the Mannlicher-Schonauer rifle was, however,
very badly made, as the narrow end of the case
often split, which might leave the bullet in the
bore and spill the powder-flakes in the breech and
magazine. (Since above was written Brig.-Gen.
R. Pigot has inherited a baronetcy and is now
Brig.-Gen. Sir Robert Pigot, Bt.)

In 1913 I first began to correspond with John G.
Millais, and we exchanged many letters, mostly
about big game, although a few were about wildfowling and sport in Britain. He was a most able
field-naturalist, and a fine shot and an experienced
angler. He wrote and illustrated many books
on game, flowering plants, and travel, and although
it is one of the smallest volumes he wrote I like
best his *Wanderings and Memories*, a volume dealing
with his early life and later travels abroad. He was
a great friend of Selous and Neumann, and probably
knew a greater number of big-game hunters and
naturalists than any man of his time. He, like
Selous, had a very fine museum of trophies, but
unlike the latter did not mind adding to his collection specimens he had not himself shot.

I think he was one of the most generous men I

ever met, for before I met him he sent me a copy
of his book, *The Wildfowler in Scotland*, and later
gave me a coloured print of his picture : " They
Cannot Break His Sleep," done in memory of F. C.
Selous. I have a letter about this picture which
I will give a little further on. Then one day I
received from him the gift of another print, " The
Last Trek," a picture by his father, Sir John E.
Millais, of a hunter dying near his wagon on the
veld, with two natives sitting near him, and a herd
of zebras in the distance.

Another gift I got from him was the book
Wanderings and Memories, because it contained a
chapter on Arthur H. Neumann, in whom I was
interested. His elder son, Capt. G. de C. Millais,
Bedfordshire Regiment, was killed in the war,
as was Selous's elder boy, Capt. Fred Selous, M.C.,
R.A.F.C., and they were both young men who,
had they survived, would doubtless have made a
name for themselves in sport and natural history, as
their fathers did before them.

It was in 1913 I first began to correspond with
J. G. Millais, and his letters were mainly about
wildfowling, round the coast of Scotland, which,
as a whole, he probably knew better than anyone
else. Here is the short letter about his picture.
" They Cannot Break His Sleep," in memory of his
friend F. C. Selous. It is interesting because he
explains how the picture was used by the Government in the war for propaganda purposes, and
where the artist got the idea of drawing it.

" (Compton's Brow, Horsham, Sussex, 29/12/20.)
    " I send you a good reproduction of my picture,

'They cannot break his sleep,' as I think the subject will appeal to you.

"I saw the grave of an elephant hunter in East Africa in such a situation, and the lions roaring at night gave me the idea of the title.

"The Government used this picture during the war for propaganda purposes in the colonies, and published 50,000, but it was badly and cheaply reproduced. Now the firm which got this reproduction done say it cannot be published except at a loss, so sent me six complimentary copies so that some day I hope you will find it is valuable. With best wishes.

(Signed) "JOHN G. MILLAIS."

The print, in colour, depicts two lions on a rocky hill-side in Africa with the hunter's grave above on the skyline, and is a most effective picture. Selous was really killed in undulating bush country, and not on a bare hill-side, but the scene has no pretence of showing the actual place of his death. As Millais only got six prints it was a most generous act on his part to send me it, and to add his signature and date on the margin.

With regard to his father's picture, "The Last Trek," he told me that he was the model for the dying hunter. I have heard people say that the figure was that of F. C. Selous, which is a mistake.

One of the longest and most interesting of Millais's letters was written from :

" (Compton's Brow, Horsham, Decr. 20th, 1918.)

" I have been absorbed in a great big Buffalo picture. Red Indians hunting them in the old days of which I saw just the end, and when I get interested with my subject I let correspondence go to the devil, as there is nothing so interesting as creating wild scenes of the game life in the past as well as the present, and though for the most part they are unprofitable, and I fear often inadequate, it gives me some joy in knowing that few artists have seen these scenes and can put them on paper for future generations. Loder showed the only buffalo pictures done by men who saw them in great numbers at the time—1865 to 1880, and they struck me as feeble and amateurish, and he suggested I should have a go at the subject, and I have already finished one with about 1000 buffalo in the picture, and am now trying a more ambitious subject, though with figures and horses it is far more difficult.

" With regards to your comments—I only suggested in my book that Finaughty was the greatest English hunter of his time and so he was. Certainly the Boers, Viljoen, Jacobs and P. Swartz killed more elephants than he did, and I have said so. By and bye as you are so interested in Neumann I will send you what I have written of his life. He was a charming and deep character, but very sociable to anyone who knew him well and they were very few. I never knew a more lonely man, or one more suspicious of friendship. It was quite

a long time before he seemed to like me, and then
he opened his heart abundantly and gave me of
his best. He was subject to dreadful fits of depression, especially in England, in crowds which seemed
to obsess him, and to affect him more than they
did Fred Selous. Most unfortunately no one was
with him in one of these depressing periods and he
shot himself.

"I have heard Selous state that —— claimed
too many elephants ; and more than one contem-
porary hunter has told me that although he killed
a lot he grossly exaggerated, therefore his evidence
must be received with caution.

"The only thing I have against Roosevelt,
who is a delightful man and a personal friend, is
that he has an abominable habit of being photographed with every zebra and Kongoni he shoots
for the pot as if it were some great feat. Personally
I loathe these wretched amateur photographs,
and of the successful hunter posing in front of
mangled corpses. It is of no earthly use or scientific-
ally instructive and gives no correct representation
of the animal, whilst it displays a cheap conceit
which future generations will only laugh at, and
say as in Roosevelt's case : 'Here is a book dealing
with the chase and habits of wild animals and there
are 57 illustrations, nearly all from amateur photographs and the author appears grinning beside a
carcase in 53.' I think it is deplorable.

"I am sorry I don't recollect your wife's father,
but think I had some correspondence with him

about poor Jack Pinckney's tombstone, but I may have met him in those now alas far off days; then I did nothing but shoot wildfowl. I have walked three times round the coast of Scotland from Dunbar to beyond Thurso, but my favourite ground was the Tay estuary and the Western Islands. I killed all the wild birds it was possible to get and used to shoot ducks for the pot as well. These were grand days, and when I was 15 I used often to go to Monifieth, and sleep out on the sandhills by Buddon Ness, and so on to Arbroath and north-wards.

" You are quite right, Anderson should be spelled Andersson. He was a Dane. I doubt if I shall ever tackle the subject you suggest re past-time hunters and their exploits. Selous could have written such a book well, and I know of no one else who could do the subject justice. I know nearly all the present day hunters and did know a few of those of the past, but nearly all the old-timers are dead. Still I know of one place in Africa where even to-day game is as plentiful as it was ever in South Africa in the old days, but it is well hidden and far away, so I do not think it will be spoiled for some time yet.

" It is very hard to get a good moose nowadays. I have killed some good ones, but for every one I believe I have tramped 100 miles—Caribou are easy if you can find them, but the good ones always leave ground visited by hunters. I have some splendid specimens. No, I have never seen Gordon

Cumming's and Steedman's lists of their trophies
and should much like to do so. I have seen most of
Gordon Cumming's heads, and he had no remarkable
ones except Scottish Roe and Red deer, and two
marvellous White rhino horns which I got photographed for Ward. (See his book on ' Records.')

" I knew Oswell slightly, he was, as you say,
a splendid man, and I also knew Stigand fairly
well (he showed me his heads the other day at
Eastbourne, and had one grand Koodoo), but I
do not like his writings or his patronising remarks
on other sportsmen. There are many other hunters
who shoot on the plains (which he despises) who
are quite as good hunters as he, and they look
upon the game in its proper perspective. Because
a man's views do not agree with yours that is no
reason his ideas are wrong. He perhaps has a
different standpoint and interest, and to say that
bush shooting is the only one worth doing is all
bunkum. I know for a fact from a man who has
lived the last four years (in close intimacy with
Stigand) that natives found all the game for him
as they do for all white hunters—Selous or anyone
else included (though many species of course one
can kill without their aid) ; so he talked nonsense
in adopting his very superior tone. Not that I
mean to suggest Stigand is not an excellent hunter,
he probably is, but I don't like his tone with regard
to others, or even beginners who must shoot on
the plains to commence with, if only to learn their
rifle. After all he was a novice himself once.

"Mrs. Selous had some idea of giving her husband's collection to the Nation, but the last time I saw her there was a hangfire.

"Yes, I have some fine trophies. Most of them I have shot myself, but a few of the best were given to me by friends, and I have never refused a superlative head just because I did not kill it myself. As a man like yourself well knows we may shoot a great amount, and never kill a record head, although fine specimens; but I have been unusually lucky and worked hard especially in North America and Europe, so I have here some grand specimens. My collection of deer heads is I think unusually fine, and I should like to show them to you some day. The following are a few of my best:

"*Moose.* I have killed two 57 and 61 inches. Cassiar on to borders of Alaska. The larger is a very fine specimen, but not as good as those of Kenai. I have also one of 65 with immense palms given me by an old friend.

"*Caribou or Reindeer.* Two very fine specimens from Cassiar, one 57 inches long. Another short, but very massive of 53 points. One record head from Labrador killed by an Eskimo 67¼ inches long and very thick. 35 Newfoundland Caribou, four first class up to 49 points, 4 Norwegian Reindeer, one good 54 inches, one long and thick 53 inches (Arctic Norway, I shot him in 1916, when I was British Consul at Hammerfest) and 2 others, good.

"*Red deer.* 5 from Carpathians of which two

are good 14 pointers. A large number of Scotch and one Norwegian Red deer good.

" *Roe.* I think I have the best collection of these in British Islands up to 12¼ inches.

"*Mule deer.* One record head, and another good. White-tailed deer only fair.

" All the usual South and East African game.

" *One Koodoo*—63 inches—I think the best head I ever shot.

" *Sable antelope.* Good up to 45¼ inches. I also possess a presented head from Angola 61½ inches. A marvellous specimen and very thick. [Later Millais got one from Angola of 64 inches.— D.D.L.]

" *Buffalo.* Two good ones up to 45 inches across.

" *Roan antelope.* Fair.

" *Impala.* Very good 31, 30, and 3 of 28½ inches.

" All Hartebeests and small antelopes as usual.

" *Dorcas gazelle.* North Africa 13¼ inches. This is good.

" *Grizzly bear.* A fine one mounted whole. I got this in·Cassiar, also Black bear, and in Norway a good specimen European bear.

" These are some of my best and I should like to show them to you some day.

" Well, I have written you a long letter, and my picture is dry so I can get to work again.

(Signed) " JOHN G. MILLAIS."

The Jack Pinckney mentioned was an Englishman of a good family, who had become poor, so he came with a brother to Fife and worked as a professional fowler on the estuary of the River Eden. Millais mentions a lot about him in his book *The Wildfowler in Scotland*.

The Gordon Cumming and Steedman lists of African specimens are very scarce, but I happen to possess both, given me by my father, and I sent them to Millais to see, and he was much interested in reading them.

Millais's remarks about Stigand running down the plains sport in British East Africa are a bit pungent, but here I agree with what Stigand wrote, for except that plains shooting needs accuracy in shooting there is little true sport in it, and it cannot be compared to bush hunting, where the art of tracking comes into play. Also, I cannot agree that Stigand had all his game found for him by natives, as from personal experience with him in Nyasaland I know he could spoor himself when necessary.

Of course, he (like myself) was not as expert as really good native trackers, but we often proved that we could compete with average ones. Really expert native spoorers are few and far between and take some finding, as I know.

With regard to the late Colonel Roosevelt and his shooting exploits when he went to Africa, and his liking to be photographed standing over his harmless victims, there was a scathing reference about him by Sir Frederick Jackson, K.C.M.G., C.B., in his book *Early Days in East Africa*, where he remarks in Chapter XXVI, page 381 : " It was, however, a matter of great regret to learn from

Col. Roosevelt's own showing, and from others, that he was so utterly reckless in the expenditure of ammunition, and what it entailed in the matter of disturbing the country ; and that he so unduly exceeded reasonable limits in certain species, and particularly the White Rhinoceros, of which he and Kermit (his son) killed nine, etc."

With regard to the expenditure of cartridges practised by many Americans—in 1911 I happened to follow the trail taken by an American party, and the empty cartridge-cases lying about the veld reminded me of places I had seen in South Africa during the progress of the Boer War after an engagement had taken place, for they were often as thick as peas. This is hardly playing the game as it ought to be played.

When I visited Millais's museum I was mostly interested in his moose, wapiti and caribou heads, probably because I had never had the opportunity of shooting any of these species of game. I forget whether he then had the record Angolan sable of 64 inches, or if he obtained it afterwards. There are two heads in existence of this race of sable antelope measuring 64 inches on the curve, and Millais's is the better head, as the circumference of it is 10¼ inches and tip to tip 23¾ inches, against 10 and 19¼ inches for the other. His son Raoul went to Angola after these sable, and shot four lovely specimens, measuring 59½, 58½, 56 and 54 inches, which Millais mentions in a letter from Cannes to me in March, 1926. As at that time these sable were being much hunted, I think it was a fine feat for a young man to obtain such splendid heads, and showed that he must have exercised great perseverance and shot extremely well. It is anything but easy, when one gets in range of such a fine trophy as a big Angolan sable antelope, to keep one's nerves steady enough to put in a killing shot, for even the oldest hunter in such circumstances might develop a fit of " buck fever." Raoul Millais accompanied his father on his Sudan trip, and did some very nice pictures of antelopes, which appeared in his father's last book, *Far Away up the Nile*. These drawings are exceptionally life-like and he promises to be a fine artist. In one of his letters to me, written from Cannes, Millais mentions meeting an Admiral Hunt, who once, in Africa, killed seven lions in a few minutes.

He also met in Nairobi in 1913 a young Boer transport-rider named Postma, who, he wrote me, killed nine lions—also in a few minutes. I always understood his bag was seven. I met this Boer, Postma, in the following way : I had left Deepdale Drift, in Kenya, and was trekking back towards Kijabi on my way to Nairobi, and thence back to Nyasaland. My tent was pitched near a water-hole close to the road, and I had finished my evening meal and was sitting in my camp chair smoking, when I heard the rumbling of wagon wheels and the cracks of the driver's whip.

When the wagon came in sight of my camp fire, which threw its light on the road, I stepped over to see who it was, and got into conversation with the Boer, who told me his name was Postma. His slightly younger companion was also a Boer, who did not seem to understand English well. I said to Postma : " Give your oxen a breather and you both come to my tent and I shall get you some tea." They stayed about an hour and then trekked on to Deepdale Drift which I had left that morning.

After I had got back to Nyasaland I got a letter from a friend in Kenya (then B.E.A.) telling me that Postma had rested his oxen there, and had just inspanned when a troop of thirteen lions attacked the oxen. Postma jumped on the wagon, and with a ·350 Rigby-Mauser started shooting, and killed seven of them and wounded two others, which got away.

Perhaps my correspondent made a mistake and he killed nine. Anyhow, seven was enough to please anyone. None of the oxen seem to have suffered more than a few scratches, as the yoke-skeys on their necks partially saved them. The evening Postma and his companion had tea with me they had a big mongrel dog with them of the Great Dane type, and I have since often wondered what part he played in the scrimmage.

When I had stopped at Deepdale Drift I had spent some time walking through the surrounding bush in the hope I might get a shot at a lion, as I had heard that it was a good place for them, but never saw a trace of them. Yet here was a Dutch-man, who probably had no wish to be bothered with them, killing a great number from the top of his wagon.

In North-Eastern Rhodesia I met a man who had come out on a shooting trip who in a week or two after leaving Fort Jameson, shot two fine elephants he had seen when walking along a road.

Regarding lion shooting—plenty of men who had been in lion country for years never got a shot at one, and some novice just out would run into them at once and get one or two.

In some of his letters Millais refers to Africa, that is, wilder Africa, as " the land of romance," and he is right. There is always a pleasant touch of sentiment in his writings, and he always chose expressive titles for his books and paintings. For instance, what can beat *A Breath from the Veld* for his first book on African sport and travel, and " They Cannot Break His Sleep " for his picture in memory of his friend Selous? The title of his father's picture of the hunter dying on the veld is " The Last Trek," which also displays a nice feeling. To those who have really felt the glamour of the wild and primitive such touches of sentiment appeal greatly, so long as they are not overdone and become too sentimental.

Besides shooting abroad in Newfoundland, Western America, and in Africa, Millais took much interest in home sport and natural history, and his writings show how much he studied the birds and animals of Britain. Here is a letter dealing with a few of these subjects from :

" (Compton's Brow, Horsham, 21/12/20.)
" It is very kind of you to send my children a Scotch bun of the old type I once used to remember in my youth at Perth. They have already had a party and have made themselves all ill on the strength of it.

" I am glad to hear you have had a visit to Loch Spynie. It is a wonderful place, especially in the winter and spring. That and Loch Leven are certainly the most interesting wildfowl resorts in Scotland, and whether for sport or natural history they have no equals in Great Britain. Jimmy is quite as wild as he always was, and an interesting character unlike other men.

" I had three weeks' stalking from Sept. 20th to Oct. 14th this year, but the weather was shocking, until Oct. 10th and then magnificent.

" At Ardverikie I got 12 stags, and shot two with very good heads the first day, but after that saw nothing remarkable till I got to Fealar on Oct. 14th, when I killed a nice thick 10 pointer, the best of the season there. It does not bother me to go out with a stalker now as they are usually such nice men, and if they find you know the game you can practically do exactly as you like, at least that is so in the two places I usually go to. One season at Fealar I killed 20 stags in a fortnight by myself, as there was only one stalker left, and he went out with other men, and I found it made little difference whether I had a man or not because I knew every yard of the ground. One day this year I went all through to ———— alone, and saw about 25 big stags, but nothing to tempt me to kill one.

" Nowadays you do not see a head in Scotland worth taking home once in a hundred stags, they have much deteriorated of late years, as the winter of 1917–18 killed off nearly all the big stags in Central Scotland.

" The Highland stag is worth stalking only for the fact that he is very alert and really requires care to approach. All other conditions such as curtailed marches, etc., spoil the sport, and only make it a favourable substitute for the real thing. But for a young sportsman it is the best training there is, as it teaches a man the vagaries of wind, and the necessity of having an eye for ground, so that the approach can be done out of view of all those prying eyes.

" My wife is so averse to my going abroad, and at present the cost of any expedition to good places is so enormous that I have no plans for the present until things get better, but I live in hope of taking my son, who is very keen on the rifle, for some hunt in East Africa, or the Thian Shan, before I get too old and stiff. I can still ride and walk all day, but get tired sooner. Yesterday I got back from Cumberland, where I was laying out a large garden, and had two nice days at cock pheasants 73 and 62, and 10 and 5 woodcocks. In Decr. I had a very good shoot in Norfolk 800 wild pheasants in two days. A wonderful place where they rear no game and everything wild and flew well. I got 72 pheasants at one stand which was quite pre-war. I don't care for this sort of thing often, but I find that a big blatter keeps one's eye in and makes one quick.

" On Jan. 4th we have our International Spaniel Field Trials near here and there will be some good dogs. I get about three days a fortnight here with the gun, but for the most part it is just shooting and not game finding, and the former is so much inferior.

" I spend most of my time when not working

at some book or picture, at gardening, and getting ready for the spring. We have a magnificent collection here of flowering trees and shrubs from America, China and Japan, about 5,000 varieties, and it is a delightful and healthy occupation.

" My book on travel and big game of N. America at which I have worked on and off for 30 years was refused by ——— ; the first book ever turned down owing to expense, but I shall keep it, and wait for better times rather than have it murdered on the cheap. A book on Magnolias also refused, so I shall just go on painting and getting ready for another exhibition.

" In July I go again to Ardverikie where I am ornamenting with forest scenes a complete house. I did 20 last year, and hope to do 20 more this next summer.

" I hope to see you one of these days at Broughty Ferry. With best wishes to you and your wife for Christmas, and many thanks for your kind present.

(Signed) " JOHN G. MILLAIS."

The Jimmy mentioned in the first part of this interesting letter is Capt. James Brander-Dunbar, of Pitgaveny, near Elgin, the owner of Loch Spynie and some fine shooting ground. He has been much abroad, and there are few men living who have shot in more parts of tropical Africa or know more about the game. He is an excellent shot, and a most interesting character to meet, for to anyone who has lived in the wilds it is pleasant to know a man such as he, who can be thoroughly natural, and without the insipid conventionality which is so common among the people of this country who have not travelled in primitive lands, and " who only England know."

When staying once with the laird, where I got some fine fishing in Loch Spynie, I was interested in a curly retriever he had which used to lift trout into the punt out of the water without marking them in the least.

One of the finest (if not the record) roebuck heads was shot in the Pitgaveny woods, with fine length of horn and beautifully long and curved points.

This is a great country for wild geese in the spring and the laird and his keepers get their full share of them, but it is dirty and wet work ditch-crawling to get round them for a drive.

In *The Wildfowler in Scotland* Millais gives a long account of Loch Spynie and its bird life ; and the place is also mentioned in Charles St. John's *Natural History and Sport in Moray*, published by David Douglas, Edinburgh, in 1882, including a most excellent heliogravure of the loch with the old castle beyond.

To return to my letters from Millais, he writes from Fealar Lodge, Enochdhu by Blairgowrie, on April 26th, 1923, that he is going to Ardverikie for a fortnight's stalking, and mentions that he has shot 6½ brace of ptarmigan at 3,000 feet and about 12 brace of grouse on his way home that day. Then he mentions a trip he proposes going to the Sudan with his son Raoul, where, as he puts it : " They want me to write up Lower Nile re-

sources—Big Game, natives, etc., like Newfoundland." He hopes to get Mrs. Gray's antelope and
specimens of Derbian eland, sometimes called
giant eland, although their bodies are no bigger
than the common species of eland found in South-
Central and Southern Africa.

After getting home he wrote me an interesting
letter about his stalking at Ardverikie.

"(Compton's Brow, Horsham, 20/10/23.)

"It is very kind of you to send me your new
book and I shall read it with great pleasure. Hunting
books always fascinate me. . . .

"Just back from Ardverikie where I shot 18
stags in 14 days and got the best head of the season,
a fine strong 10 pointer, 35 in. long which is good
for Scotland nowadays. I saw a wonderful sight
on Oct. 1st, 400 big stags all the stock of Ardverikie
in one corrie and all roaring together, but the
stalker wouldn't go in the corrie though he had
no valid reason for refusing—such is Highland
deerstalking to-day with its silly restrictions.

"My boy Raoul also killed a very fine royal at
Fealar, the best for six years.

"Awfully pressed as I leave Dec. 1st for Port
Sudan, and do not know how to get through the
proofs of my Rhodo book. Also I have an exhibition in London (Fine Arts, etc.) all November,
have also to lay out 2 gardens, and have 2 Field
Trials—some work, but no doubt will resolve
itself into order with a little management.

"I will write you a good long letter if I have any luck in South Sudan. Many thanks for your excellent hints, they are much appreciated. Best wishes to your wife.

(Signed) "JOHN G. MILLAIS."

When he returned from his Sudan trip he sent me the promised long letter, which was most interesting, but his writing was very shaky, for he had been seriously ill. He was always so busy with one thing or another that he often wrote in a hurry, so his writing at its best was not easy to decipher. This letter was difficult to read, but here it is, and I believe I have puzzled out his caligraphy correctly :

"(Compton's Brow, Horsham, Sussex, 22/4/24.)
"I promised you a letter about our Sudan trip, but I cannot write a long one as I should like as I am far from well.
"R. and I had a very nice short trip to Red Sea hills for Ibex, but of course we got wrong information and went to hills played out by local Arabs constant hunting so no old bucks.
"We got 4 all right, but only moderate heads, also 8 Isabella gazelle and 3 Salt's Dik-Dik, one a record.
"Ibex driving was wonderful and very skilfully managed, but shooting difficult as Ibex came galloping by anything from 100 to 300 yards. However, we killed all the best we saw.

" Camels are nice to trek with. You only want a very few to carry provisions for a month.

" Then down the Nile for 1000 miles to ―――― bottom edge of the Great Swamp. Then in 80 miles, and we struck north into the wilds to Mrs. Gray Swamp. We found them at once and killed our 4 in two days. I got a beauty nearly 33 inches and very thick. The hunting was severe, up to your middle in swamp, no cover and pursuing a buck that saw you approaching all the time. I got a very good one just at sunset at 300 yards and was devoured by mosquitos as I took the head off. Then S.E. over ―――― plains where we got White-eared Cob, Vaughan's Cob and one old buffalo bull. I could have shot him but gave shot to R. who made a lovely shot moving at 250 yards and knocked him down. He was apt to be wicked so our natives and gunbearers took to the trees. We walked up to him and R. killed him nicely with a shot through spine. After this I did not bother about my son as he is a finished hunter already and I think without prejudice the best shot I ever saw. He killed 7 gazelle mostly at 300 yards in succession.

" Then South and we got Roan, Henglin's Hartebeest, Warthog, etc., after which made for Rumbek where dysentery attacked me. We were now in a quandary as close to Giant Eland country. R. refused to leave me so next day I got on my donkey and went off. It was pure Hell for 3 weeks and no milk in Juer country near the Gelle. In

8 days I found Giant Eland fresh spoor and R. went out and killed 2 bulls next day having luckily picked up the only Dinka hunter in the country who could really spoor. The herd ran when he found them but R. ran parallel and when big bull (38½ in.) came clear killed him dead. Then he ran 3 miles (108° in shade) going right away from the natives and killed second bull at 280 yards. Next day R. killed 2 fine buffalo bulls and made back to Rumbek when dysentery suddenly stopped and I was quite well. Then same night I had a bad attack of malaria which continued in virulence for a month until I was carried in collapse into Khartoum Hospital where a wonderful doctor completely cured me in 5 days.

" Now I am all right and though weak and tired am rapidly picking up. On the whole we did well in spite of troubles, but I shall always regret I did not kill a Giant Eland myself. Yet the next best thing is to see your son do it properly. Giant Eland now *very rare*. Several of the old known herds extinct by cattle plague. I expect they will be on closed list.

" I could easily have got a White Rhino but Sudan Govt. would not grant one.

" I hear you have met my old Uncle George. He is a dear old boy. Hope you and the wife flourish.

(Signed) " JOHN G. MILLAIS."

This is a most interesting account of a hard trip

in a very hot country and I fancy Millais was getting rather old for such strenuous work.

The kindly remarks he makes about his son shows his fine sporting spirit, as it must have been a great disappointment for him to be laid up just when they had reached the eland country. To anyone who knows the conditions of African hunting, and the keenness a young man would feel when he got within range of such fine game, it shows that R. Millais was a remarkably cool and fine shot in doing the work his father describes. And to run after game in such blistering heat is also a proof of great endurance.

I have often run after elephants and other game, so I know what it means to cover three miles of rough country carrying a rifle and ammunition. It is pleasant to think that there are still hardy young men left among the many softies one sees in the younger generations.

In his interesting book, *Far Away up the Nile*, Millais gives some of his son's drawings of game, and they are about the best I have seen, as the artist has made his animals really life-like. It is wonderful how art runs in families and sometimes comes out in succeeding generations. I have often wondered if animals which are seen to exhibit exceptional wariness in a herd may not have inherited this quickness in detecting danger, for there is no doubt that some individuals of a certain species are much " quicker in the uptake " than others.

With regard to visiting sportsmen in the hunting-grounds of Africa, I remember an interesting discussion I had in 1904 with two men who were exceptionally fine hunters. My friend Martin Ryan, whose death I record in previous pages, had returned from a hunting trip in the region of the Luangwa river, and had put up his tent and made a camp on the border of a stream outside Fort Jameson. Barns, later well known as a hunter and collector, and myself had walked over to see Ryan and, by invitation, have an evening meal with him, which consisted of some good hartebeest steaks, scones and tea. After our repast we sat by the camp fire and talked about Ryan's experiences on his recent trip, and the conversation came round to hunting in British East Africa, and the high fees white hunters got for taking out a party. Someone, I forget who, made some slighting remarks about these visiting sportsmen who would have lost themselves if they had strolled alone for a mile into the bush, and took home trophies sometimes shot by their white hunters, and so on.

In the conversation I remarked that there were "Visitors and Visitors," and mentioned J. G. Millais and Abel Chapman—who were not only very fine naturalists, but most interesting writers. I remember saying : " Look here, we three are so accustomed to seeing and shooting game that we get stale, and the fevers we get, and bad food we eat at times, all reduce our strength and therefore our capacity for observation. Men who come from Britain are fit as we were when we first came ; their brains are acute, and they sometimes see things and note them when we do not, because we are so accustomed to seeing them that they do not strike us as being remarkable."

It was seldom that I went with others to hunt as I always preferred to be alone where there was nothing to jar one, for unless Europeans know each other very well and have exceptionally good tempers under the stress of hardships and rough travel, one is better to be independent. Most African hunters are men of great self-reliance and individuality, so they do better work when they are free to go and do what they like and are not worried by the talk and actions of others.

That evening I remember well, for as the dusk of day faded into a purple darkness, with the stars showing and a fine moon, the camp fire threw its beams on the green tent, with the heads of game grouped on one side, including the grinning, half-cleaned skull of a good buffalo head. We were all fit and hard, and Martin Ryan had a long, scrubby, tawny beard, and his face, arms and legs were as brown as a chestnut. Barns, like us, was in shorts, but instead of going about in bare calves he wore putties made of white calico, considerably stained with mud. This caused the natives to call him "The Stork," for he was quite six feet in height and had very thin legs. We were all good walkers, and thought nothing of tramping twenty-five or more miles in a day, and keeping this up for days on end if necessary. Near us the natives were busy eating their evening meal of "nsima" (porridge made of mealie flour), and one could hear their teeth tearing the meat Ryan had given them.

The moon, instead of throwing silver beams earthwards, in Africa has a golden tinge—why I do not know, but it is a mistake in Africa to speak of the "moon's silvery light," as we do in Europe if we wish to be poetical !

Sitting by a camp fire in the African bush with natives and game trophies about always made me feel romantic, and the memory of that evening, simple as it was, recalls the glamour Africa used to throw on me, and its everlasting lure to those who love the wild and primitive. It also reminds me of the mutability of life, for now Ryan and Barns have gone, and the places and men who knew them will know them no more.

Men who are fortunate enough to be able to go for trips after big game, when they are naturalists trained in the country life and sports of Britain, have a great advantage over men who live for many years in a wild country in Africa, because they have the advantage of study of the latest news and literature on the subject, and the opportunity of seeing the specimens sent home to the big museums, and meeting men who have shot in different countries. One cannot expect them to know quite as much about the game, or how to track it, as the man who lives in the wilds, when he is an individual who makes a speciality of the subject, but, as I have written, he brings a fresh mind to bear on the subject and is usually in the best of health.

Somewhere in his writings, I think in *Wanderings and Memories*, Millais points out that sport in Britain can also entail dangers. Punt-gunning is a cold and often dangerous amusement, and so is mountaineering, as witness the recent loss of two young men in the Cairngorms of Scotland, these being additional to another two men lost about five years ago. Such fatalities are usually due to foolishness and recklessness, and men who take such risks often suffer if they face arctic conditions insufficiently clad. It is just as easy to break one's neck deerstalking in Scotland as it is when following markhor in the Himalayas, or wild sheep in Alaska, if one falls over a precipice, or puts one's foot on a slanting

slab of stone when crossing a scree slope with a
long drop below. Regarding bodily risks at home,
anyone who motors much is in constant danger
from beginners, or reckless drivers.

But after this long digression I must get back to
my main subject of the letters. Millais writes me
on June 22nd, 1925, about the matter of an animal
called the "Chimpekwe," in N.E. Rhodesia, which,
I believe, is completely extinct, although I think
it must have been in existence in the early years of
the 19th century for I have heard the natives talk
of it but never met one who had actually seen one.
They say it had horns on its face like a rhino and was
as large as a hippo. It may be a myth, but if so
it seems to me strange that a name (or rather several
names in different parts of Africa) should be used to
describe it.

Millais, too, mentions the great heat in the
Bahr-el-Ghazal district of the Sudan, and agrees
with me that although he has never been there,
the Zambezi valley must be as bad, and I am sure
it is, if not worse.

Then I got a letter dated January 18th, 1927, full
of interesting matter on some controversial subjects
which, being confidential (though it is not marked
so), I cannot give. In it he again mentions a big
book on American sport and travel which he has
had waiting for a publisher for fifteen years.
Apparently he could not get suitable terms, or make
arrangements for the type of paper, and quality of
the illustrations. He also regrets that a well-known
early work of his was not produced in a better way,
and says his knowledge then was not so great as
it is now with regard to the quality of the paper
used by publishers.

Millais was an excellent shot with a catapult, and as I have used one of these things since I was a youth I wrote and asked him how he made his, and got the following interesting letter which is the last letter I ever got from him.

" (Compton's Brow, Horsham, 14/6/28.)

" I don't see anything to criticise in the material you use in small catapult. (1) Fork, bag (of old glove), elastic and shot are all right and much as I always used to use. (2) Of course, a heavier shot requires heavier elastic. You must test it and see which shoots best.

" 3. Yes. In small catapult I only slotted the fork carefully, and sandpapered the edges so as to prevent chafing.

" 4. I used a pouch a little larger than you figure.

" 5. Length of rubber depends on whether you wish to take long or short shots. Usual length for close range 9 to 10 inches.

" 6. I always hold the fork in right hand.

" 7. I used to get the rubber from local man here, but have not used a catapult for two years. If I can get some I will send it.

" 8. Keep rubber warm in trousers pocket for 2 days before using.

" I think the whole art is perfect combination of touch, hand and eye, and most of all judgment for allowing drop of the parabolic curve in flight of shot.

" To shoot well you must be very sensitive, be

in good health, and do your final jerk (which gives force on impact) at the right moment without altering aim.

" I return your sketches and I think they are about right. Yes, the ——— Museum are the limit in stinginess and stupidity. I am not surprised at their refusing to exhibit your unique specimens. That is why they have only a moderate collection.

" I am glad you like Moffat so much more than Peebles.

" Our garden has been good lately with heaps of Azaleas, Rhodos and Wisterias, etc., and now with copious rain the growth for next year is good.

" With best wishes to you and your wife.
(Signed) " J. G. MILLAIS.

" PS.—The Broughty Ferry creeping genista is doing well and now fine big clumps."

The remark about the big game specimens referred to an offer I gave of several trophies (some the record of their kind) to a well-known museum on condition they would be exhibited in perpetuity and not put away in a cellar or store. This condition, for some unknown reason, was refused, so the museum in question did not get the specimens. I have heard of fine trophies being presented to museums, well worth exposing to view, which have been valued so little that they are put away out of sight.

Millais was a most kindly man, and he helped many young sportsmen, and from what he told me did not always get much thanks for it.

He was a fine rifle and gun shot, a most observing field-naturalist, a fine artist and an interesting writer, not to mention his other varied accomplishments such as his growing of flowering shrubs and his art in landscape gardening. There have been few men who had greater knowledge of the game birds and wildfowl of Britain and Europe, and regarding big game and its natural history his opinions were exact and sound.

The "Life" of his friend Selous is one of the best Biographies ever written, and not the least interesting part of it is the illustrations done by himself. One (p. 144) of a herd of African buffaloes stampeding is most life-like, and on p. 240 is a charming picture of an American Wapiti roaring defiance in a forest. This is one of the best nature pictures I have seen in a book. I miss his interesting and kindly letters.

CHAPTER V

Norman B. Smith

I NOW come to the letters of my friend Norman Bayley Smith, who is one of the best sportsmen I ever heard of, for he is supremely moderate on his shooting trips, and believes in sparing all but the best heads. Considering how shamefully many men (who cannot be called " sportsmen ") behave in Africa it is a pleasure to know that there are still men left who believe in " playing the game " when they go on a shooting trip, with a long list of animals allowable on their licence which they can kill at will. N. B. Smith does not do this, for he is extremely careful in selecting his heads, with the consequence that he gets excellent ones, and does not slay a lot of small stuff, as do many others, which are only fit for the rubbish heap.

The first letter I got from him was from :

" (Kiel House, Ardgour, Argyllshire, 21/9/1912.)

" Your note to ' Mannlicher ' was forwarded on to me from the *Field*. A lot of nonsense is written about the dangers of photographing the heavy game. There is, of course, as you know, very little danger except in the case of wounded game. I have crawled about with a Kodak amongst elephant, rhino and other game, but almost the only photo I ever took that incurred any danger was one that I took of a rhino in 1900, as I was anxious to get an interesting photo for my lantern. This rhino 'rushed' me as I was walking up a game path through 5 ft. grass on the slopes of Mount Kilmaine. I was carrying a ·303 with my Somali behind with my 10 bore black powder rifle. I blazed at its face and jumped to one side, and it swept by and down the hill. I afterwards found the ·303 split bullet had gone through the front horn (a 22 inch horn) about six inches from the top causing it to hang back. The rhino went into a patch of reeds, so I had a chance for a Kodak snap, my Somali keeping at my elbow with the 10 bore on cock. I went to about 25 yards of the reeds and shouted. He came out slowly, at right angles, and I got a good snap showing the broken horn. As I twisted away the film, backing away as I did so, he swung round and I got a second snap that gives him at about 30 yards with all four feet bunched together in his stride, head down and horn horizontal. The 10 bore stopped him. That is the only risky photo I have taken, and photos of unharmed game are practically devoid of risk. I fear I am writing you a long letter, but I believe people don't mind them in out of the way places.

" I have shot off and on (in Africa only) for the

NORMAN B. SMITH

W. D. M. BELL

last 20 years, and there are few heads worth having
that I still lack.   I have been in most parts of Africa,
but not in Nyasaland, though curiously enough
I half thought of going next summer with Bayley
Worthington, a cousin of mine, who is anxious
to go there, an excellent shot, who has done well
with Ibex and sheep, but has only done East Africa
in that greatest of all big game countries.   He for
a long time held the Ibex record with $57\frac{1}{2}$ inches.
No, I have written no books except that by request
I wrote the big game section in a Stock Exchange
sporting book called *The House on Sport* 12 years
ago.

" Certainly quote my note of last April if you
wish to.   As regards a possible visit to Nyasaland
there would be many heads that B.W. wants,
but few if any that would be new to me, though
I am always ready to ' improve ' in a variety I
already possess.   I am a bit of a ' crank ' on the
subject of the slaughter of game that takes place,
and am always urging that the limits imposed since
the days of licences are not strict enough in many
cases, also that it is quite needless to kill the full
limit.   I make a practice of never killing any good
species, unless I think the animal has a better head
than I possess, and having once got a specimen
new to me I avoid killing another till I get a real
good one.   Thus with many trips done I have only
shot 3 eland (best Ward's measure $31\frac{1}{4}$ in. × $13\frac{1}{4}$
circumference) ; 4 Sable (best 50 in. though it was
$54\frac{1}{4}$ in. when shot) ; 5 Roan (best 32 in.), etc. ;

and though I have seen many of these species since I obtained my best specimens I have not shot at them. If I want meat I look to my pal's trophies to supply it, or I shoot a wildebeest for the men, or an oribi for myself.

"As regards Nyasaland I still lack both Nyala and Situtunga. I have not a good bushbuck in my collection, nor curiously enough a really good buffalo. Perhaps I might obtain both these, but I fear the more desired Nyala and Situtunga would not be there.

"Is sleeping sickness much of a risk there now? Any information you can give me I shall be very grateful for. My permanent London address is: 13, Beaufort Gardens, S.W., but the Conservative Club, St. James's Street, will always find me.

"Perhaps when next at home you will let me know, and we will meet to have a yarn together.

"Walter Conduitt has just been staying with me. He is a cousin of your friend Stigand.

"I was in Barotseland in 1905, but have not been in Rhodesia since, but have been working up the Soudan heads with three trips, and only lack the Addax and Derby Eland there now.

(Signed) "NORMAN BAYLEY SMITH."

His remarks in this interesting letter about the dangers of photographing big game are in full accordance with mine. Most of the pictures one sees of game "charging" are pure rubbish, as in numerous cases the angle of the animal shows that it is not exactly facing the camera, and an animal when it charges advances in a straight line and does not swerve much.

Now follows an excellent letter about game slaughter which it would do "butchers" much good to ponder over, and again I agree with what the writer says :

" (13, Beaufort Gardens, S.W., 15/12/1913.)

" I am sorry you won't be up in town for some time, but I hope when you do come up that I shall be in town myself. I could, of course, arrange for you to see my heads in my absence, but would vastly prefer to welcome you in person and talk ' big game ' over a magnum of the best.

" I have abandoned my projected trip to B.E.A. with a friend leaving England on the 30th, but I may go to the S. of France in February for 3 or 4 weeks for a change, as I have not been quite up to the mark the last month. I shall be here all January except an occasional day or two shooting. When you have some idea of the probable date you will be in town, let me know and I'll fix up a night. I'll try to get my cousin Bayley Worthing-ton to dine the same night, as in the event of your trip to Nyasaland next June coming off, he might like to join you. He has often asked me to go there with him next summer, but as I have all the species near there except Sassaby, and the buffalo are poor, I have no object in going there. A first class buffalo head is now my objective though

I should also like to get Situtunga and Nyala some day, when I should with their inclusion lack little of note in Africa. Also I prefer leaving England in the winter months if possible. B.W. is a fine fellow, a 1st class shot, has hunted in Africa twice and in Ibex countries several times. I introduced him to the sport, consequently he is the reverse of a butcher. As regards buffalo I believe B.E.A. is a surer find for a wide-spread head than Uganda. They have increased largely in B.E.A. the last few years, and heads of from 45 to 48 inches are got very frequently by men who look before they shoot. The Game Warden assures me that I should be certain to get one over 45 inches (my *pons asinorum*) seeing that I should be working solely for buffalo, so would devote plenty of time to finding the right thing.

" As regards my strong views on killing heads one can't want, solely for the pleasure of killing, and, of course, making allowance for the necessities of meat, but when a man exhibits a photo of —— —— shot at the same time it is obvious he is a butcher and doesn't realize it. If I ever had to kill so many at a go for the sake of meat I should greatly regret the fact, and should certainly not advertise the deed by a photo. There is this difference with pheasants ; they are in no danger of extinction, for they can be replaced ' *ad lib.* ' according to the purse of the proprietor and all are used as food. I have not a word to say about shooting meat for carriers, or for starving natives, I only ask the sportsman not to overdo it, to utilize the commoner and uglier species such as hartebeest, and when shooting meat for *natives* to shoot *old males*. The man I am down on is the ' Sportsman ' who shoots down 4 or 5 from a herd, probably mostly poor heads, takes the best head or two, and a good piece of meat from one of them, and leaves the rest for the vultures.

" In B.E.A. 14 years ago I had 70 porters, and of course had to shoot some meat, but when meat was required I shot hartebeest or zebra, and never shot the finer species for that purpose alone, though when I shot them for the sake of a good head I always tried to get all the meat in. ———, a great hunter, I believe, was a terrible butcher on his own showing, for to kill or wound 5 or 6 buffalo (regardless of sex) in a few minutes could never have been necessary on the score of meat. In your case meat must have been a constant need, and from your writings I feel sure you did not abuse it. Although there are many butchers amongst men who go to Africa solely for sport, I fear the local white man is often the worst offender. Fifteen years ago very few men went to Africa to hunt, now their name is legion ; but thanks partly to my crusade in the *Field* against butchery, and similar views expressed by various good sportsmen, the novice has nowadays a good idea of what he ought not to do. The local man is often far from any control, and shoots anything and everything, and is a butcher without realising it, or surely a man like ——— would not have circularized the Shikar Club with such an abomination as his circular.

"I fear I am boring you with this long letter mostly on the one subject, but I have such strong feelings on the subject, and am so anxious that this splendid variety of game should be saved from extinction—that was such a blot on South Africa and in America.

"I don't know who ——— is in the *Field*, but I have given him in next Saturday's issue some pretty straight truths on his continued advocacy of rifles being sighted for shooting game at 500 yards.

"Please excuse this long scribble, and let me know when you are coming to town.

(Signed) " N. B. SMITH."

There is no doubt that if we had more sportsmen with the moderation the writer of above letter displays that the future aspects of the game would be better than they are to-day, as it cannot be questioned that many men shoot much more than is necessary or fair. The grand hunting-grounds of Southern Africa were denuded of their fauna by the meat and skin hunters, and several species were exterminated. Central and Eastern Africa probably have a greater variety of antelopes than did South Africa in the old days, and so long as they remain they should be conserved for our future generations of sportsmen, naturalists and nature lovers. Apart from the cruelty and vandalism of extirpating such beautiful creatures, as many of them are, it would be a false policy in other ways, for the game from elephant downwards are a most valuable asset on account of what it brings to the several administrations which control our dependencies in Africa.

The next letter I give also deals with game preservation, or rather the actions of those who believe in slaughter instead of conservation.

" (13, Beaufort Gardens, S.W., 11/12/13.)

" You will remember we had a short correspondence some while back. I hear you are now in England. When are you likely to be in London ? Will you let me know and I shall be glad to fix up a night for you to come to dine quietly with me here, and have a chat on the great sport, when you can see the pick of my African collection, which I have in this house. I have not room for many duplicates so in most species I have merely the best head on view with a few duplicates of the handsomer species. The one notable species in which I fail badly, is I regret to say buffalo. B.E.A. is the place to get fine buffalo now, and I was by way of leaving England on Decr. 30th, for B.E.A. to get a good buffalo, by good I mean well over 45 inches. However, the man who wanted me to go with him doesn't want to go as far afield as I do, so I decided this morning to postpone the trip till next winter. Thus I shall be in London this winter. If you are in London next week, or any time in January I could fix up a night.

"In all the trips I have done I have seen large numbers of most leading species, yet I have only shot 3 or 4 of each, never killing except what seemed a better head than I possessed. Result—out of 4 Sable best 46¾ and 50¼ inches. Eland of 3, the best 31¼ by 13¼ circumference. Lesser Kudu of 4 the two best were then 1st and 2nd records, the best still 1st ; and so on in other varieties. That should be the hunter's aim, quality not quantity.

"When I was in B.E.A. the buffalo were practically extinct from rinderpest, and the best I saw I did not consider worth shooting at. Nor in Rhodesia did I find one worth setting-up. Thus I have only a good Nile buffalo on view, but I hope to remedy this next winter in B.E.A.

"I shall look forward to meeting you and having a yarn on this grand sport. Hoping you may find a date convenient. You will have noticed I have been 'going for' the folk who advocate pumping lead into animals, or around them, at 500 yards.

(Signed) "NORMAN B. SMITH."

Most good sportsmen will agree with the contents of this letter, and the writer was quite right in censuring the photo I gave in one of my books of five lechwe which was lent me. Not having a good print of a single lechwe with a fair head I used it, but like N. B. Smith I think it is slaughter to kill a lot of immature heads.

Certainly when one has a large number of natives

to feed, and keep happy, one has often to shoot a good deal of meat, but when this is so one should always kill the commoner and least handsome animals such as hartebeest, waterbuck, zebra or warthog.

When a man gets into a country where the game is very abundant one does not imagine that what is killed will make much difference, and neither it does, perhaps, in a single case, but if everyone goes on the same plan when many are shooting the fauna will soon be reduced in any locality. Then in the case of rare species a man will think : " If I do not get it some one else surely will." So to make the game safe everyone has to act with moderation, and restraint on the part of a very few individuals will have little effect in the preservation of animals.

However, " every little helps," and the example of the few often induces decent sportsmen to be moderate when they happen to be men susceptible in a moral sense. But there are many who are greedy and ruthless, and no amount of ethical precept will have any effect in changing them. With such " killers " the only thing they can understand is to suffer in their persons or pockets, which shows that to conserve the fauna one needs the supervision of wardens and rangers, plus legislation to award punishment of a kind sufficiently drastic to be a certain deterrent. Unfortunately the cost of proper supervision is expensive, and in a large district a lot of poaching and slaughter can go on without anyone hearing of it.

Sometimes a young man who is keen and excited lets himself go when he gets in range of a herd, and may wound many more beasts than he kills.

The hunter can only follow one animal at a time, and if the shooting takes place late in the afternoon, or evening, the wounded game are then unlikely to be seen again and finished off.

At the end of the letter quoted there is a remark about rifles sighted for 500 yards. This is really quite unnecessary as the great majority of the shots will be taken within a distance of 150 yards. If not they certainly should be, for much beyond this range it is impossible to see the angle at which an animal is standing, and when this is so one should not fire. Only on three or four occasions have I shot at game at more than 200 yards, and I remember killing a hartebeest at about 300 yards, and two elands at about the same distance, all with a single shot, and I took these long shots to get much-needed meat for my carriers and boys, and for those of a friend who had arrived with a large following and had camped near me. To make a practice of long-range shooting at game, especially in bush and undulating country, shows that a man is incapable of stalking. Really one sight for 150 yards is all that is necessary on a modern rifle, and with " Magnum " small bores a single sight will be regulated for 200 yards and be good up to 300 yards.

My old .256 clip-type Mannlicher has a standard, three leaves, and a tangent up to 1,200 yards. I hardly ever raised the first leaf marked 200 yards so why a rifle should be fitted with so many unnecessary sights is more than I can explain, unless such a number is meant to make a weapon suitable for military purposes !

After this digression I will get back to N. B. Smith's interesting letters.

" (Conservative Club, St James's Street, S.W., 22/3/1916.)

" Many thanks for the book which I have read with much interest. I would like to keep it a few days more as I wish to copy out some notes and comments from it. It is well written and there is much that is sportsmanlike, though I think the excellent condemnation of pheasant shooting as compared with naturally wild birds is somewhat negatived by the admitted habit of pumping lead at a running lion up to 500 yards. You know my views on running shots at harmless game ; I hold them in a much less degree also as to lion, etc. I hate to wound and lose a lion, for many years past the wound would grieve me more than the loss, unless it was a very fine beast.

" In the chapter by my friend Butler of Khartoum one man is quoted as having wounded 9 lions and got none. This man was probably a bad shot, and certainly must have had poor nerves, or he would have got close enough to some of them to make certain. In my first Somali trip in the early nineties I wounded and lost two lions, each time after a long spoor, and each time an awkward shot. Both of these I followed up through thick bush and high grass, alone save one gunbearer, without being charged or getting another chance. On that trip I killed four, and have killed lions since in various parts of Africa, including a second visit to Somaliland, but since that first trip I have skinned every lion I have fired at, and have always refrained from firing at lions galloping away even at much closer distance than ——— always pumps lead at, and have refrained from killing moderate lionesses on two or three occasions when I could watch them undisturbed, as I didn't wish to destroy them, nor the trouble of skinning them, nor even wanted the skins, and certainly didn't want to add to my numerical bag.

"I have killed two exceptional lions, one Somali, the other East African, of which the late Rowland Ward said I might hunt twenty years in Africa and never get, or see such a pair again; and these like my finest heads have made me not very anxious to kill any more inferior specimens. I have given away all my lion skins except these two, which are mounted under glass—head and shoulders.

"You will have read the anecdote in the book about Capt. Renton's shikari being killed. I arrived on the Somali coast for my second trip just after this occurred, and took on Hassan, the surviving shikari, who guided my caravan to the place where the event occurred, and described the spoor of this huge beast so accurately that when at last we found the spoor (the only one fresh or old I saw in the district) it was clearly the same lion, and after about eight hours' spooring I killed him in the most exciting (though perhaps unwise) bout I ever had with a lion. Not long after I gave an account of this incident in the *Field*, and as it may interest you I enclose the cutting, which you will perhaps kindly return when next you write. It relates the incident exactly as it happened.

" To return to the book, I think there is far too much talk of lions charging. Rainsford is quoted as saying : ' 19 times out of 20, when a lion charges he does so and so.'

" I don't believe any living man has seen 20 lion charges. Lions don't make a ' hobby ' of coming at you, or the good men at the game would kill far more lions. Again, I think that any man who has often been charged by lions must be either a bad workman, or else in the habit of pumping lead at unwarrantable distances.

" Inverarity was a great character as a big game hunter, and I am glad to hear he is still alive.[1] If you quote my views to him as to ' charging ' I fancy he will agree. Sitting up at night for lions I regard as a miserable way of getting them, only excusable for a man anxious to get his first lion. Hunting them with dogs is scarcely fair, as it gives the lion very little chance, and almost eliminates all danger. Riding them with ponies is exciting, and perhaps legitimate, but doesn't give the lion much chance. I did it once, and rounded-up and killed three in a few minutes, but have never done it since. I am more pleased to have killed a moderate number single-handed and on foot, by tracking or by stalking than I should be to have killed three times the number by night or with dogs. Perhaps I am a ' crank ' on the subject, but the ' motive '

---

[1] Mr. Inverarity has died since this was written.—D.D.L.

is I am sure right. —— thinks lions take a great deal of killing. My weapon for them has always been a ·577/·500 blackpowder 'express,' shooting 6 drams powder and a 440 grains bullet, with copper nose and small hole at point. With it I have found that when I get a fair chance the first shot leaves small chance of a charge, and the second precedes the skinning. Small bore magazine rifles will kill lions if hit absolutely right, but I think nothing much under ·400 should be used when after lions. If I knew I was in for a lion charge I would rather have a shotgun with big shot, A.A.A., or S.S.G., than any rifle, and should not fire my 1st barrel till he was within 20 feet. I don't think he would reach me.

"To return to your letter I shot a Sable in N.W.R. eleven years ago, which measured 50¼ inches. It was also so measured by Capt. O'Sullivan, and Commissioner Dale, before I left the country, but had shrunk a trifle when it reached Rowland Ward's, and they made it exactly 50 inches.

"Stigand's Kudu must be magnificent. Yes, B.E.A. for a really big buffalo. I have set-up one buffalo head, a massive and good specimen of the Nile buffalo; for my best specimen of the true Bos Caffer, though slightly wider was not so good of his class as the Nile one for his. Some day I hope to kill a real good one in B.E.A.

"My ·256 is the old pattern. My only other rifles have been a heavy 10 bore 'Paradox' for elephant and rhino, and the ·577/·500 blackpowder for lion, etc. The last of the few elephants I have shot I killed with a ·400 cordite lent to me, as I had sold my heavy ' Paradox.' If I went again for elephants I think I should take a Jeffery ·475.

" Well, I hope this very long letter won't bore you, and with many thanks for the loan of the book.

(Signed) " NORMAN SMITH."

It will be seen from the above that the writer takes a great interest in the measurements of trophies, and that his ideas on fair hunting methods form a good lesson for the novice, and those others who are not beginners whose main object is the " bag " and not the way the animals are hunted.

With regard to the shooting of records there is sometimes much luck connected with the getting of first-class heads, as they are often got by pure chance. In the above letter there is the mention of Stigand's fine koodoo which I looked after for him when he left Zomba to go up to Fort Manning near the North-Eastern Rhodesia border. Stigand shot this fine koodoo (63⅝ inches curve of left horn) in the Liwonde district when on a short trip from Zomba, and he told me that when he had stopped for a moment or two to look round in the bush he suddenly saw this animal without knowing its head was so good. He fired at it, and after a finishing shot got it, and was surprised to find it had such a grand head. It was the finest head of a koodoo I saw all the time I was in Nyasaland and Northern Rhodesia, but it was certainly got by chance, and anyone lucky enough to come on it could have bagged it—that is to say, if he had shot straight. Many other records and superior trophies have been got in the same way. I suppose the way to judge a collection of trophies is to consider the average size of the lot in comparison to the usual measurements of each species. To pick and choose, as Norman B. Smith always did, shows that it took a lot of patience and perseverance to make his collection.

The value of a head depends very largely on the incidents connected with its hunting, especially with dangerous game, when the hunt may finish up with a " scrap." For instance, my favourite buffalo head is very poor for width, the right horn has been slightly broken, but the horns are big on the bosses, and he was a fairly old beast. I value it because I hit him at dawn one morning, and followed him steadily for six hours through thick bush and long grass in absolutely blazing heat. At the end he put all my men, except my gun-bearer, up trees, and I finished him on foot—the last shot being fired at a distance of exactly nine paces. Therefore, his mortal remains bring back the memory of his pluck and gallant end, and I would rather possess his headpiece than the record from Africa.

Sometimes a specimen is good for a certain district, but may be inferior in another. Take the sable antelope, for instance. In Nyasaland, North-Eastern Rhodesia, and in other parts this animal inhabits, a head of 42 inches on the curve will be quite good. Yet in Portuguese Angola this species grow horns up to 64 inches, probably because there is something in the feed (phosphates) which tends to exceptional horn growth. Therefore, a trophy has to be judged by the locality where it is obtained.

With regard to the use of small-bore rifles for lions, such as the ·256 Mannlicher, I have always been a believer in small-bore rifles, because they are so accurate and light to carry in the great heat of the tropics. One has to shoot accurately with them, but so one has to do with a large bore if an animal is to be killed. The shock (striking energy) conveyed by a big bore is useless unless it strikes a vital spot, so one might as well use the more accurate small bore, which gives one a better chance of putting the bullet in the proper place.

The ·577/·500 blackpowder "express" which Norman Smith used for lions is an excellent weapon, as the lead bullet with a small hollow in the point is certainly good for soft-skinned dangerous game. Selous shot many lions with a Gibbs'-Metford rifle with a 360-grain bullet, and even occasionally killed rhino and hippo with the same kind of projectile. The worst point about black powder is the smoke of the discharge and recoil, although the latter is hardly felt in "express" rifles under ·577 bore. Blackpowder 4-, 8- and 10-bore (so-called "elephant" rifles) were a different matter, and some of them "kicked like mules." I once possessed a single 4-bore which shot 12 drams and 4-ounce bullets, and also a double 8-bore by Boswell and a double 10-bore by Purdey. The 4-bore, on firing it, nearly jumped out of one's hand, for it was rather light for such heavy charges. I soon gave up these old-fashioned weapons when I found how pleasant and accurate were rifles like the ·303 and ·256.

When I was a tea-planter in India (*circa* 1895)

I thought of buying a double 8-bore to use on a trip up the Bramaputra River, beyond Sadiya, after buffalo, so wrote to a Forest Officer who had a double 8-bore rifle I had heard he wished to dispose of. He, when passing near the garden, brought along his weapon, which was by a good maker and in excellent order. I did not know so much about rifles in those days as I learnt later, so when we had put down a wooden box, with a bull's-eye marked in the centre with a lump of charcoal, he loaded his fearsome-looking tool, cocked both triggers and handed it over to me saying : " Take plenty of time and shoot slightly low." I think (though I forget exactly) that it had about 12 drams in each barrel with conical bullets.

I had recently had a good deal of fever, and was under nine stone in weight, but this does not affect the recoil if one leans well forward and keeps one's muscles relaxed, and a heavy man often feels recoil more than a light one. I aimed low and fired, and was astounded at the result, for the rifle flew out of my hands, and I described a back somer-sault, and arose with a sore cheek and a big bruise on the back of my skull. The F.O. by this time was cursing freely, as he had picked up his cherished " blunderbuss," which he was stroking with a red and green "bandanna" handkerchief to remove the dust. The stock was scratched slightly, but the weapon was otherwise intact. This hammer 8-bore had done exactly what nearly all these rifles did when both triggers were cocked, and I have never understood whether the F.O., being a bit of a wag, wanted to see some fun, or whether he forgot the fact that his rifle had this fault by cocking both locks instead of only one. However, he was a bad salesman, for I did not like the weapon, though afterwards, as I have mentioned, I possessed several of the kind in Africa. I believe it is a fact that when these large bores are made with hammerless actions they seldom develop this tendency of jarring off the second lock.

Once when shooting wildfowl on the estuary of the Tay River, on a cold winter's day, with my hands numb with frost, I touched off both barrels of a heavily loaded 12-bore. I was smoking a pipe with an amber mouthpiece, which snapped off in my mouth, with the result that I nearly swallowed it. This, of course, is a different matter from one lock making another go off.

The next letter is from :

" (13, Beaufort Gardens, S.W., 4/4/16.)

" Thanks for return of *Field* cutting. The story does not confirm my belief in the ·500, but this is easily explained. When I took the first shot from the brilliant sunshine outside into the dark lair, where the lion was, I really couldn't make him out properly, only a dark mass and a tail tip twitching above and beyond, distance perhaps 10 or 12 yards. I afterwards found that this shot was not central enough, just catching the shoulder bone near the point, and breaking it without entering the body. A few inches more to one side would have meant a miss. This entirely due to the darkness making it impossible to locate the lion properly, my aim being guided by the roaring

of the lion, and the position of his tail. ——'s
rifles are not bad. I have had several, my ·500
and my Mannlicher, and two rabbit rifles. All
you want to do is to test and adjust the sights.
I have never even fired one of the pointed bullets
which were so much discussed a few years ago.
I believe in a big bore cordite for elephant, ·450
to ·500. My armchair cogitations (before I had
tried cordite rifles on elephant) led me to the conclusion that with them the first shot should if
possible be aimed at the 'point' of the shoulder,
or centre of the big shoulder bones. Such a shot
would I think eliminate all danger and would
secure every elephant so hit. I have only had one
chance of experimenting, when with a borrowed
Jeffery ·400 cordite (rather a small bore) I completely crippled with my first shot an elephant bull
on the upper Nile. This shot breaks the shoulder
bone, and the animal can neither pursue nor escape.
My experience with elephants is very small, four
attempted with blackpowder rifles and one with
cordite—all killed. Before I ever hunted them
I studied the skeleton in the S. K. Museum, and
satisfied myself as to vital shots. The same applies
to rhino, eight attempted and all killed with blackpowder, so I have no suffering cripples on my
conscience.

"You will by now have received back the Lion
book with my best thanks. What do you think
of my comments ? Though not necessarily right
they are my own well thought out convictions.

The question of the right bullet (as to solidity) for each class of game is I am sure the right road to success.

(Signed) " NORMAN SMITH."

Personally I prefer magazine rifles, but their misuse often causes suffering to the game. No magazine rifle is as well balanced as a single falling-block or double rifle, but in many ways they are superior, such as in the reliability of the striker pins, which hardly ever go wrong, as do the nipples in singles or doubles. Then the fact that one has five shots at one's disposal is a great advantage when hunting dangerous game. After the two cartridges in a double are expended it takes time to reload, likely at a time in the proceedings when every moment is of the greatest consequence. Therefore, a magazine rifle may save one's life, or enable the hunter to put in a quick finishing shot, which eliminates the necessity of following up and finishing an enraged animal in thick country. However, this has always been a controversial subject, and, of course, everyone can use the weapon he prefers. The great thing is to know one's rifle well, so the one used oftenest is likely to prove the most successful should a hunter have several to pick and choose from.

Referring to shots for elephant, and the allusion to the shot at the " point " of the shoulder, it has always been my belief that this is much too high, as the heart lies very low in the cavity of the chest. One-third up from where the line of the body passes between the forelegs is the place to shoot at in a dead broadside shot. This means the bullet has to penetrate the nearer leg-bone, so it is better to be slightly behind the elephant and put the projectile in the soft part behind the leg. I have written this many times, but wish to emphasize it as often as possible, as I know of many fine elephants being lost through the hunter shooting too high. Lately I bought a book entitled *Elephant*, by Commander David E. Blunt, which is one of the best works I have read on the subject of elephants and their hunting. The plate facing p. 142 shows the spots for the brain and heart shots. The former is correct, but I believe Commander Blunt has put the mark for the heart shot at least one foot too high.

In Volume XIV of the Lonsdale Library, *Big Game Shooting in Africa*, in the Frontispiece, and on the plate facing p. 99, I believe I have marked the heart shot correctly from the position the animal is shown in the photograph. When marking such spots on a picture one can only represent the matter from the angle shown, and when there is time to move round in the actual shooting one would naturally have occasion to pick something better, so as not to risk a bullet being turned off by striking the rounded bone of the leg.

In the letterpress (p. 99) I put the following sentences regarding the effect of the brain shot, which needs a little explanation. I thought of it afterwards, but too late to correct in the proofs. I wrote : " The result of a correct brain shot is final, as the elephant collapses in his tracks. Should an elephant, after falling, make the slightest movement, it is best to run in from slightly behind, and put one or two bullets into his ear-hole ranging forward." In these sentences I forgot to mention the muscular spasms which usually follow a brain shot, and show in a quivering of the body and extremities. Sometimes there is no sign of this, and when it does occur it does not last long, as after a few seconds the contraction ends in a final shiver which shows that the animal is dead.

The remarks by Commander Blunt on "Elephant Control" in Africa are most interesting. There was no such thing when I was out there, and it was often noticeable in outlying villages what an amount of damage the herds did to the natives' crops. In fact, I have known of cases when this almost caused starvation at times, and I have several times shot meat for the hungry people. This book of Commander Blunt's should become a standard work on the subject, for it has been written from much practical experience in the field, which, after all, is what really counts.

There is much difference in the methods of hunters when they fire at elephants or other dangerous game. Some take extreme care with the first shot, and watch the result before firing again, while others, after shooting, believe in putting in several shots in quick succession with the idea that should the first bullet have failed to get the vital spot aimed at, some of the subsequent projectiles will do so.

Barns once told me he often fired his full magazine into an elephant, and then loaded up quickly by using the charger made for Mauser rifles. Others have written they do the same at a lion, and there is no doubt that such a bombardment would likely quell any desire of a dangerous beast to charge, whereas it might be more ready to do so after receiving a single bullet which might have missed the vital organ and made it furious with pain.

Elephants hit in the body are more liable to be nasty than those hit in the skull, when the brain has been missed. No real sportsman can object to an animal resenting an injury and trying to get at' its enemy, but again no hunter wants to be smashed by an elephant or buffalo, or be mutilated by the teeth and claws of a lion or leopard, which are poisonous in the highest degree.

After this usual digression I come to another interesting letter.

" (13, Beaufort Gardens, S.W., 7/4/1916.)

" Thanks for your long letter. Certainly wild-fowl, duck, geese, snipe, etc., and then grouse and partridge provide far more real sport than pheasants.

" *Running shots*—You know my views. A wounded animal may be fired at as long as there is reasonable chance of a hit, but I always prefer to let them go, give them a rest, and then follow up.

" *Lion charges*—Are less liable in the case of a man on foot, as the lion knows he can probably get away. Rainsford's book I have, and I think it is very nicely written, but assumes too much on a small experience. I am rather conservative in all things, and my liking for blackpowder rifles is because when I started hunting in Africa they were (magazine small bores excepted) the best available, and I was very successful with them. The smoke is a nuisance, but with my ·577/·500

I could put most shots in a 6 inch bull at 100 yards, and never fired at anything over 150. I used a 480 grains solid, or a 440 grains hollow, so the hollow point only reduced the bullet $\frac{1}{12}$th of its weight. My old Mannlicher has never jammed.

" As regards S.S.G. for a possible charge, I should not fire my first shot till the animal was within ten yards, when the shot would drive right through the skull. A ·400 cordite is fairly powerful, and is the only heavy cordite I ever fired at game, having borrowed one and shot one elephant and two buffalo with it, but a few shots with it at antelope with small lead nose bullet were very disappointing, the bullets passing through (broadside) without setting-up.

" *Bullets*—With the ·303 and ·256 I always used Jeffery splits, and they killed all antelope, including eland most successfully. I only fired two such ·256 at two eland bulls, about 140 and 130 yards, killing each with one shot. One fell at once, the other ran about 150 yards and then collapsed. It is possible the split bullet in the large bores would break up too easily, owing to the weight of lead inside the envelope, but I have no experience.

" If I again hunted lions I should use my old blackpowder ·500. If I take a ·470 cordite for buffalo to B.E.A. I will experiment with it here on carcases with expanding bullets to see which should be best for say lion or soft-skinned animals. For buffalo I should use Dum-Dum type. I once tried my light 12 bore ' Paradox ' at a waterbuck at about 120 yards. I hit him three good shots before he gave in ; one such shot with ·256 split bullet would have downed him. The 12 bore ' Paradox ' is a bad gun for lion except at very close ranges, i.e., inside 30 yards, as the 3 drams powder doesn't give half enough drive.

"I think Sandbach lost his life partly through this. I wrote at the time that a 12 bore for lion should fire a minimum of $4\frac{1}{2}$ drams. I was on the scene of the disaster shortly after, and had the incidents explained by Hirsi Shirch—the boy who killed the lioness on the top of Sandbach. It was a story of very bad tactics, poor shooting, and that with a gun lacking drive. It was his first and last lion.

(Signed) "NORMAN SMITH."

When I get a letter from a friend mentioning rifles I cannot refrain discoursing on a subject which has always appealed to me. I have possessed a large number of rifles of different bores and types, and am a strong believer in magazine weapons, for various reasons formed from practical experience of game shooting in Africa, and some of which I have already mentioned.

The great thing is to get to know a rifle thoroughly, and the one most used, naturally the small bore for killing antelopes, etc., will be that tool. There are several important desiderata, which I would class as follows :

1. Lightness.
2. Accuracy.

3. Reliability.

4. Cheapness.

Therefore, there is no double made, even by the best of makers, which can compete with a magazine rifle in these respects.

One of the best books on rifles is *Notes on Sporting Rifles*, by Major G. Burrard, D.S.O., a work all should read who are interested in this subject. Having shot a lot in India, where double rifles seem to be more popular than they are in Africa, Major Burrard recommends doubles.

Of course, everyone can use what he prefers, but I never saw a double rifle I would like to carry all day long in the roasting heat, and through the rough bush of tropical Africa, where every pound towards the end of a day feels like three.

Doubtless when one is fresh and cool a best double by a first-class maker is a most pleasant weapon to handle as it is probably nicely balanced, and its weight, of say 10½ lbs., is hardly noticed. But transpose the scene to the Luangwa Valley in north-eastern Rhodesia on an October day, when the sun is blazing out of copper-coloured molten sky like the glare of a blast furnace! Moreover, imagine that it is afternoon and the hunter has been on his legs since dawn spooring an elephant through thick bush and grass, with no water at hand, and his throat dry with the fine dust from the ash of a big grass fire which has swept through the country. Then, if one wants to add a further true touch to the scene, suppose the hunter has had a recent " go " of fever, and is feeling ill and weak, and is suffering from disappointment in not being able to overtake his quarry, which always tends to make a man more tired than when he has been successful, it can easily be seen that lightness is a most important feature in a weapon. Some people will say that a gunboy can easily be got to carry the weapon, but those who have had the greatest experience of gunboys are generally those who do without them and carry the rifle themselves. Of course, one often takes out a spare rifle, but all good hunters believe in always having a weapon in their hands, as it is usually at the most unexpected moments that chances occur.

The weight rifles are made mainly depends on their calibre, and therefore the bigger they are in the bore the more they weigh.

Then when we consider the next clause of " Accuracy " (No. 2) there can be no doubt that it is easier to shoot straight with a small bore than it is with a large. Further, good shooting largely depends on practice, so it is natural that when a man has used a rifle much in shooting the small mammals he will do better with it when he comes to shoot the largest of game, such as elephants. The most important thing is to use the right type of bullet for each species of game. For all the antelopes I think the best projectile is the " Dum-Dum," which has a small bit of lead showing at the point, and nothing can be better for a lion than this pattern. It will also be quite capable of killing rhino, buffalo and eland with side shots and even facing shots, although I think for those beasts solid bullets are more reliable. For head and body shots at elephant, and for head shots at hippo, solid bullets are essential.

Regarding " Reliability " (No. 3) I think magazine rifles are far superior to doubles, even when the latter are of the highest grade, for it has been my experience that the nipples of doubles are sometimes liable to break, and the lock-springs fracture. With a magazine one seldom hears of a striker-pin breaking, and I only once heard of a spring weakening and causing occasional misfires. A double when opened in heavy grass or bush may get a tiny bit of vegetation between the barrels and action, which prevents the rifle closing if fitted with a top or side snap lever. Therefore, although old-fashioned, the pull to the side bottom lever is much more reliable as it exerts so much force that the barrels can be closed. In double rifles or single falling-blocks never have an automatic safety bolt. Any gunmaker will soon make an automatic bolt into the more practical non-automatic, and it might save a man's life in a " tight place " to have this done, for I have heard of fatalities through a sportsman forgetting his rifle was " on safe," and finding that it was unfireable when charged at close quarters.

I do not expect everyone to agree with these comments, but they are at least founded on knowledge of the subject.

As to my last clause in favour of magazines, i.e., " Cheapness," this word should not be associated with nastiness, for it is often true that some cheap things are nasty. It is my opinion that a well-made magazine action is a wonderful bit of mechanism—the result of great inventive genius, for in comparison to the fairly complicated locks of a fine double rifle the lock of a Mannlicher or Mauser is a simple and wonderful bit of work.

When fitted with the ordinary single pull-off, regulated fairly easy, it enables a man to do excellent shooting if he can remain steady and cool in risky situations. The extended, or drag pull, when the trigger comes back a little before the striker is released by the final squeeze, is, in my opinion, an awkward device, and invariably put me off my shooting. The first dangerous animal I tried this rifle on was a fine bull buffalo which I had spoored with two others at dawn. Climbing a big anthill, I saw his head and neck projecting from some thick grass, so instead of taking my Rigby 7·9 mm. Mauser, which I had out with me, I decided to try the shot with a Jeffery ·404 fitted with this drag-pull. With my Rigby at the distance of sixty yards or so I could have got him in the neck, and expected to do this with the ·404, but I didn't, for at my shot the bull (which was accompanied by two others) gave a grunt and bolted. The cool of morning soon blazed up to torrid heat, and I followed a thick blood spoor for quite six hours, getting several shots at the tough beast, once knocking him on his back, though he was up in a jiffy and off again. The two other bulls had soon left him, which, of course, made the spooring much easier, as there was no chance of losing it.

I was determined to get him and put him out of his pain, but considering the amount of blood he dropped I could not understand how he was able to carry on. My shorts got quite red with the gore off the grass and leaves I brushed against in the chase. To make a long story short, I eventually brought him to a stand, but he was a gallant beast, as he got all my men, except my gunbearer, Molilo, up trees. The latter and myself took cover behind a bush, and it was amusing to see the gallant old buffalo go to one tree, where the feet of a man hung within two feet of his nose, and grunt defiance, although the brave animal had received several bullets. I could see the blood still dropping from his neck, the result of the first shot, which had penetrated the windpipe instead of breaking his neck, as I had intended. I had the Rigby 7·9 mm. rifle in my hand, so sat down so as to get a raking shot at his heart when he stopped moving about and presented a front shot. He soon did this, and when he got the bullet he sank down, gave a few moans and expired. I paced the distance which divided us and it was exactly nine yards. On previous occasions I had cut several buffaloes open so as to examine the exact position of the heart and other vital organs, and when doing so I found that a buffalo's heart lies very low in the chest cavity—in fact, the lower part of that organ is only a few inches from the chest wall—and it is absurd for anyone to state that the heart of any animal is in the middle of the body, for it is not. I advise all beginners when they shoot game (especially dangerous game, which is the more important) to watch the cutting-up carefully, so as to fix in their minds the true position of the heart and lungs, particularly the former, as it forms the most deadly body shot. Another important place is the neck, although, unless one is very close to an animal, and it is quite still, this is a bad spot to aim for. However, it is a mark sometimes aimed at. Instead of being near the top, it is nearer the centre of the neck, being a shade higher than a medial line.

After this plucky old buffalo was dead I regretted I had given it the first shot with a rifle I did not know well, for had I used the Rigby I am sure I would have dropped the animal in its tracks, and thus saved it a painful chase, although it gave me one of the best spooring days I can remember. On getting back to civilization I borrowed a metal drill, and put in a pin in the action of the rifle, which converted it into an ordinary single pull, and I then shot better with it, but not so well as with the smaller bore Rigby.

Ultimately, getting a good offer for it, I sold the rifle to a man who liked something with a good striking energy, and he afterwards told me he liked it very much, so we were both pleased.

Some people like a rifle fitted with a hair trigger, and my old friend Barns generally used Mausers fitted with it. But I never liked the device, and it is certainly rather dangerous if one does not take great care. For instance, with such a weapon (a German 7·9 mm. sporting rifle) I had set the hair trigger to fire at a buck which bolted before I could fire. Soon afterwards, being tired and hot, I sat down in the shade of a bush, leaning my rifle against a branch. A native shook the bush and the rifle fell on the hard ground and went off. Fortunately there was nobody there to stop the bullet, or there would probably have been a fatal accident. This incident, plus the fact that I did not like a hair trigger, made me dispose of it. With this device one sets the hair trigger by pressing back the rear trigger. Then the merest touch on the front one fires the rifle, and one can set the mechanism fine or hard. To release the setting one puts a finger on the back trigger, pressing it back as in the original setting, and touches the front trigger, which converts the lock into the ordinary front drag-pull action. Then I saw a British-made rifle once, which had only the one trigger, which could be set to a hair trigger by first pressing forward the trigger. If it was not then fired the bolt had to be worked to release the hair setting, and unfortunately this did not always seem to act, as after opening and closing the bolt the hair trigger still remained set. The owner soon got rid of it, and told me it had been a perpetual source of worry to him in case someone might be killed.

These last paragraphs sound like a jig-saw puzzle, but I cannot explain the two devices more clearly in writing, although I might do so better if my reader and I were actually playing with two similar rifles to those described.

Then I had some interesting letters from N. B. Smith on war matters, and one which goes thoroughly into the matter of rifle sights, not only for big-game rifles, but for those accurate rifles made for rook and rabbit shooting at home. He believes, like me, that the smaller the front sight is the better will be the shooting which will accrue. This is certainly a point which all who use a rifle should note, if they have not already done so, as it makes much difference in accuracy.

A small antelope, such as an oribi, is blotted out with a coarse foresight at from sixty yards and over, so if one aligns a rifle on one at say eighty yards one is really sighting on the whole animal. With a front sight the size of a small pinhead one can pick the spot intended to be hit, and therefore kill it much more satisfactorily. This is one of these small matters of detail which are so important in results to the sportsman, and also in preventing pain to fine creatures.

This letter which discusses rifle sights (21/6/19), finishes with some remarks on the methods of lion hunting which are so good that I quote them as follows :

"In 1917 Percival, game ranger, B.E.A., wrote an article in *Blackwood* on riding lion in B.E.A. entitled : 'The finest sport in the world.' I wrote a reply to it in *Badminton* urging the far superior claims as to high class sport of Tracking as some of us did in Somaliland in the nineties, and pointing out that the fault of the B.E.A. method is that they dismount not less than 200 yards, fire at the lion with a small bore, and remount and gallop away if he shows any sign of charging. I maintain that if you ride them, when you dismount you should see the show through on foot, as I did with three lions the only time I tried riding them. Did you see the *Badminton*? If not and you care to see it I will post you my copy if you will let me have it back."

I had seen the *Badminton* article, but can hardly agree that B.E.A. and Somali lions are quite the same sort of animals. In B.E.A., in certain districts, lions were so much hunted on ponies that they became extremely savage, and charged at distances Somali lions never or seldom do, because in the latter country hunting them on horseback is much more exceptionable. The lion is a clever beast, and doubtless in many cases in B.E.A. when he shows signs of charging this may sometimes be bluff, and if he got going he might not carry out his attack to the end ; but again, it is, I believe, a fact that what one lion does (or pretends to do) is no criterion of the actions of the next one seen. In fact, all animals of a certain species may act differently according to the circumstances and place where they are encountered. This is why many hunters have varied experiences of the same class of animal, and it certainly adds an interest to big-game hunting that this is so, because it brings in the quality of uncertainty—in other words contrast.

A letter (13, Beaufort Gardens, S.W.3, 8/1/20) relates incidents of home shooting and then goes on to mention an experience with a chief of the Dinka race, which is interesting as it shows the worst side of native behaviour. Usually, raw natives are very civil to the better type of white man, but now and again one will come across men who intentionally try to act in an insulting way, and sometimes get away with it, unless they happen to meet a European who can assert his prestige. If the latter does so he will be more respected than one who stands any nonsense. I have had to do this occasionally, so I am in thorough agreement with the action I now quote from this letter as it was the only one possible in the circumstances.

" I was much grieved to read of the death of Stigand. I never had the pleasure of meeting him, I know he was a first rate man.

" The Shilluks are a fine race, but the Dinkas the worst in Africa. I was hunting in the Dinka country in 1909, and ' Ajok,' the local chief, visited my camp, and had the impudence to spit about in my tent after I had warned him. I took him by the scruff of the neck and kicked him forcibly out of my tent.

"Next day when out in the elephant forest with one of my men and two Dinka ' guides,' they led me into an ambush of Dinka spearmen, whom my man luckily spotted before we entered the high grass, or I might not be here to-day.

"By avoiding all thick bush and grass I managed to get back to my camp safely with my gunbearer, after several times holding them back (without firing) with my Mannlicher. We at once re-shipped tents, etc., on my ' nuggar ' and sailed north the same evening. My one joy being the remembrance of the hefty kick which sent ' Ajok ' sprawling outside my tent, though I shall never forget his expression of fury as he retired to his village.

"If things are more settled next winter I hope to go to the region north of Mount Kenia in quest of a tip-top buffalo. This is almost the only big game head of the commoner species that I have not a first rare specimen. I want a head of 48 inch or better with big bosses as well. Though I have seen a good many ' buffs,' I have never seen a ' topper ' alive. When I was in B.E.A. 20 years ago they were nearly all dead of rinderpest. Now they swarm so I might succeed.

"Re my creed of moderation I find in my diary of 1909, when I not only went up the White Nile to the Uganda frontier, but on my return north (after the Ajok incident) fitted out a camel trip into Western Kordofan after Leucoryx and Addra gazelle ; never seeing an oryx but getting an Addra almost record. My record for that long double trip was 13 head of game for 20 cartridges, including 1 elephant bull, 1 hippo bull, 1 Mrs. Gray of $31\frac{1}{4}''$ (then about record), 1 fine roan of $32\frac{1}{4}''$, 2 addra, 3 Dorcas gazelle, 3 Red front and 1 reedbuck —surely an example of moderation.

" I went out again to W. Kordofan the following winter 1910, and got two oryx, one grand head of $43\frac{1}{4}''$, nearly record. I think I sent you my article in *Badminton Magazine*, Nov., 1917, on ' Lion Spooring in Somaliland.' If not I shall be glad to send it for perusal.

" Be sure and let me know if you ever come to London.

(Signed) " NORMAN B. SMITH.

" PS.—If I could get a champion buffalo bull I think I would rest content."

Some of the trophies mentioned in the foregoing letter are very fine, and as I know from experience it is a very difficult matter to obtain first-class heads, for it entails great patience to find them, and restraint in leaving animals which may have an excellent headpiece. Some records are, of course, a matter of pure luck, but when a man's collection contains specimens most of which are high in the list one may be sure that they were the result of painstaking effort.

Next follows an interesting letter about elephants, written from :

" (Barbreck House, Lochgilphead, Argyllshire, Sep. 19th, 1924.)

" So many thanks for the elephant book which I have just finished. It will add to the collection of books on African sport in my library at home.

" As regards criticism I see little scope. To begin with my experience of elephants is very limited. I have never made elephants my objective, nor have I ever seen a good tusker alive. In the blackpowder days I shot at four elephants, three of which I killed in Somaliland, and the 4th I had a very strenuous five minutes with in very dense jungle on the Abyssinian border, the bull being ' head on ' when I took my first shot, it being quite impossible to get any other shot, as I couldn't move for thorns, and the bull was within 20 yards. I used a 10 bore ' Paradox ' in those days, and this elephant hunted for me after the first (futile) shot at his forehead, but failed to get me partly owing to the density of the jungle and the fading light, the sun having dipped ; and partly owing to his fury, as he trumpeted and smashed about all round me. Once he made me out, and advanced on me, but a second 2 oz. bullet on the forehead stopped him, and as he swung round I gave him another on the side of the head, and he fell over on his side in some terrific thorns, and lay flapping about. I couldn't get near enough to see to give him a shot on the ground owing to the awful thorn thicket, though I was within 10 yards of him but could see nothing. My Arab tracker was convinced he would

be dead in the morning, so we extricated ourselves
from this awful thicket and went back to camp not
far away.   In the morning I was down with fever
and my man came back to say he had got up in the
night and gone off, leaving a piece of tusk broken
in his fall.   They followed him for about 3 miles,
and then gave it up.   On my return journey I heard
he had been found and appropriated by natives.

" Those four are the only elephants I fired at in
my blackpowder days, the three in Somaliland being
easily killed as it was much more open forest and
I was able to get broadside shots behind the shoulder.
I have since then only fired at one elephant with a
·400 cordite.   Here I have my first (very trifling)
point of difference with you.   When cordite rifles
came in I went and studied the skeleton of an
elephant, and came to the conclusion that with the
high velocity express and hard nickel bullet the
surest and safest shot was the centre of the shoulder
bones, which would move your red disc about
$1\frac{1}{2}$ times its diameter to the left as one looks at your
diagram (page 45).   I had only one chance of
testing my theory and my first shot completely
' anchored ' the bull, rendering him incapable of
either charging or getting away.   I then walked in
pretty close to him and laid him out.   His tusks
were about the best of those I shot but were only
about 70 lbs. the pair.

" With the exception of my first elephant, which
I was naturally keen to get, and killed instantaneously
with a 2-oz. bullet through the heart, I have felt

considerable regret over all the other four except the Abyssinian one which gave me enough anxiety to eliminate feelings of compassion. I have never hunted specially for elephants, and if I had the good fortune to do further trips in Africa I don't think I should fire at an elephant unless I was tempted by a really good pair of tusks. Since my early days I have been a collector of 'heads,' a new species of antelope (with a really good head) attracting me far more than any of the heavy game. As regards the dangerous game, by far the most attractive to me was the lion hunting in Somaliland, tracking them through the thick grass and bush, most exciting work. I once got in the middle of a huge herd of elephants when doing a night march, most interesting, but I didn't see a good tusker, and didn't fire a shot. Thus, except as a theorist, my experience of them is trifling, but I think that with a cordite express, and waiting for the shoulder shot, I could kill every one I shoot at. As you rightly remark great skill with a rifle is not essential, what is needed being perfect nerves and a correct anatomical knowledge where to hit them.

"The only time I was ever injured by big game was by a rhino, but I agree with you that the risks in hunting rhino are far less than lion or elephant, while I should count lion as far the most dangerous if boldly hunted on foot in thick country. It is quite certain that far more men have been killed or maimed by lion than by any other animal. . . .

(Signed) "N. B. SMITH."

This is an interesting letter, and gives a most excellent account of hunting an elephant in really thick cover, where it is difficult to move, and when one cannot easily see the result of a shot. However, if after falling the elephant was making a noise, it was evident he could not have been " brained," as all an elephant does after being struck there is to give a few limb twitches which make no noise.

An elephant I once shot in North-Eastern Rhodesia after falling turned on its back, owing to a slight slope it was standing on, and all I saw were its four legs sticking up over the grass. I was within twenty yards, and noticed the contractions in its limbs, which gave them a quivering appearance, but this only lasted for a minute or so and then they were still.

With regard to which is the most dangerous game to hunt, this is largely a question of individual experience, and also how much each species is hunted. The matter has also much to do with personal feeling, for one man may, for some reason connected with his nerves, fear one animal more than another.

Many more men have been killed and injured by lions than by elephants, buffaloes, rhinos or leopards. Personally I think crocodiles and snakes are the worst creatures, not that I fear them more than the others mentioned. I have had narrow shaves from both, and several from the mammalia.

If one considers the most dangerous points of each creature, we could classify them thus :

Lion.
Naturally bad tempered when wounded.
Very quick in action.

Can take cover behind the smallest vegetation.
Does terrific damage in a short time.
Wounds very poisonous.
Difficult to turn off unless hit in brain or spine.
Fears man less than any other beast, and kills
many natives annually.

Elephant.
Also justifiably annoyed when hit.
Not so quick as a lion.
Usually visible unless in the densest cover.
More likely to leave a man when it gets him
down.
Wounds non-poisonous.
Easier to turn off with head shots.
Fears man much more than lion.

Buffalo.
Nasty when wounded, with good reason.
Quicker than elephant, slower than lion or leopard.
Can hide easier than elephant, owing to lesser size.
Generally most pugnacious when he gets at his
enemy.
Wounds extremely bad, but not septic.
The worst of the dangerous game to stop once he
starts.
Has a natural fear of man.

Rhino.
Usually bolts if wounded.
Owing to bad sight, is curious and blundering.
Fairly easy to spot, and is noisier when hit than
the three former.
Can damage badly owing to his great strength.
Wounds not poisonous.

Fairly easy to turn off.
Does not fear man so much as elephant.

Leopard.
Extremely plucky when wounded.
The quickest of all in action.
Takes cover like a cat, which he is.
Does poisonous damage with fangs and claws, especially latter.
Not so hard to stop as lion, but worse to hit.
Fears man greatly until wounded.

Crocodiles are sneaking brutes, and I once had an extremely narrow shave from one when standing waiting for a shot at a hippo in the muddy Bua River in Nyasaland. As I have mentioned this before in a book, I need not inflict the story on the reader, except I would like to warn novices not to enter deep, muddy water. Fishing is becoming a popular sport now in parts of Africa, and if people are not very careful, accidents are sure to happen. There is a true story of a full-grown rhino being dragged into the Tana River by a crocodile, which the late Mr. F. C. Selous mentions, and gives pictures of, in his *African Nature Notes and Reminiscences.* The crocodile must have been an exceptionally large one to be able to do this. An ordinary croc, say one of 11 feet, could whisk a man away in an instant, and once off his legs he would have no chance.

Snakes and stories about them which I could relate had I not done so before, some years ago, in the columns of *East Africa*, are so common in books and in the Press that I shall desist annoying the reader !

Unless people have had similar experiences themselves it is difficult to impress them, but I think they are a greater danger in tropical Africa than any other creature. I always killed any mamba or puff-adder that I saw and could catch, for the former species does its best to escape as a rule, and one has to chase them hard to catch them. They often stop to wait for one, and their backs are easily broken with a sharp blow. However, it does not do to miss in such a case, as they are deadly brutes.

Probably the safest and best weapon for a snake is a shotgun, but I seldom kept one in Africa, as they make too much noise, and their cartridges were heavy to carry and expensive to buy.

Another interesting letter from N. B. Smith runs :

" (Barbreck House, Lochgilphead, Argyllshire, 2/10/1924.)

" It is blowing a gale and sheets of rain, and I wish I were back in London instead of not leaving till Monday, so I am going to risk boring you by writing you on a point in your book that I think we have discussed before, i.e., your advice to use small bore magazines on heavy or dangerous game in preference to D.B. heavy expresses. I quite agree that you and I and others of experience who have thought out the anatomically deadly shots, can kill elephant or hippo by the head shot with a ·256, but I am sure that a novice should begin with as heavy a rifle as he can manage, not only for his

own safety, but also to avoid wounding and losing
these fine animals with the cruelty involved. Hippo
of course are not dangerous, so we may leave it at
elephant, though apparently you also include buffalo
and lion.

" You refer to the advantage (?) of a 5 shot magazine small bore for stopping the charge of, let us
say, elephant, rhino or buffalo over a D.B. ·470
cordite ! With the latter I believe I could stop
such a charge with far more certainty than any
man living with a ·256 magazine. Such a charge
would rarely occur from a distance exceeding 50
yards, when it is doubtful if the 5 shots could be
aimed and fired, while the cumulative effect of
them even if fired would be less than the 2 shots
from the ·470, which even fired into the chest
would I believe stop any animal. Personally I
would confine the utility of a small bore to elephant
and hippo when the head shot can be used. For
buffalo or for lion I regard their use as a great
mistake, though I would not hesitate to go for either
of them with a ·256 if I had nothing better with
me. The use of small bores for lion as a regular
thing is foolish, and accounts for the large number
of graves in Nairobi. Even George Grey, a plucky
and experienced man, lost his life in this way, for
had the two hits he made when the lion charged him
been with my old ·577/·500 blackpowder express,
with small hollow in the bullet, I don't believe the
lion would even have reached him, as the first shot,
if in the chest, or shoulders, would almost certainly

have stopped it. The open plains in B.E.A., and the use of horses led to using small bores on lion, but if any of those who in the nineties hunted lion in Somaliland by spooring on foot through thick scrub and grass had used small bore magazines, the death roll would have been considerable. Even as it was, out of the comparatively small number of men who hunted in that country, some of whom perhaps exercised more caution than I did, there were some casualties. Major Sandbach was killed, Tom Greenfield and Bontein, both friends of mine, were badly mauled, and lucky to recover. Chapman (no relation of Abel) was mauled by his first lion, and didn't try again, and I think several others, whose names I can't recall were killed or mauled. The Ingram you refer to was I think killed by an elephant in Somaliland, and from the account I heard entirely his own fault, as apparently not fancying going in to his elephant on foot he rode in to 50 yards on his pony, pulled up and shot from the saddle. The elephant at once charged seeing the light grey pony. The pony stuck its feet in the ground in terror and wouldn't move. Ingram belaboured it with his rifle in the vain hope of getting it to move, and was still doing so when the elephant reached him and killed both the pony and him.

"He was wrong to begin with in shooting off his pony, relying on it as a means of escape from trouble, instead of going in to his elephant on foot, in the correct and more sportsmanlike way; and having made this mistake he made the second and fatal one of not jumping off the terror-stricken pony when he found it wouldn't move, and escaping in the bush, which he could probably have done as the elephant would have his eye on the pony.

" As you say in your book an accident may occur with the most skilful of hunters ; that is so, but in my opinion if one knew the exact facts of all the maulings and fatal accidents, more than half of them were the fault of bad tactics, bad shooting, or defective nerves ; plus in the last twenty years, many through the use of inadequate rifles for dangerous game. Even for the best hands at the game I am convinced that, elephant excepted, magazine small bores are wrong both in theory and practice, while even the expert will have more wounded elephants on his conscience through their use, while the use of them on dangerous game by novices is extremely foolish.

" I shot all my 9 rhino with a 10 bore blackpowder killing the lot. Also 5 elephants, all killed though one (described to you) did get up and go off a few miles, subsequently found dead.

" I once met a man in the Sudan, very pleased with a fine pair of tusks—60 lbs. or more each— which he told me he killed with a ·303, but when pressed by me he admitted he had fired at some eight or nine others unsuccessfully, though presumably hitting them, for one could scarcely miss an elephant. So he had eight or nine poor wounded beasts on his conscience for one killed. He ought never to be allowed to shoot again ! An extreme instance, no doubt, but a confirmation of my views.

(Signed) " N. B. S."

I never agreed with Mr. Norman Smith about the advantage of the large over the small bore, as I have explained before that the whole question is one of accuracy and handiness. If an animal is not hit correctly with a big bore it is not killed, and it is doubtful that they are more deadly, for it is certainly harder to shoot straight with a ·470 or ·577 cordite than it is with a ·256 or ·318.

From his accounts of the number of shots he fired for animals killed I am sure he could have done every bit as good work with his Mannlicher as with any other rifle. Plenty of beasts have been hit and lost with large bores, so they are by no means infallible.

There is a most important point with regard to stopping the charge of any infuriated animal which should be remembered, and it is that no matter how large the bore of the weapon used, or the deadly accuracy of the shooting, there can never be any definite certainty that a bullet will knock out a beast sufficiently to prevent it getting at one. Elephants, buffaloes and lions have all been known to come on with a lacerated heart, and there are only three shots—all extremely difficult to place—which will entail an instantaneous collapse, and they are brain, spine and a fractured leg joint. The latter shot will not, of course, kill, but will trip a beast on to its head, when a finishing bullet will do the rest. With a small bore such as a ·256 it would be difficult to fell an elephant with a joint injury, and, moreover, such a wound would likely be the result of pure chance, as it would mean the bullet meant for the chest had gone astray to one side or the other and got a shoulder.

Certainly, when it comes to bone injuries, big bore rifles with their greater weight of bullet and striking energy have a better chance of doing damage than a small bore, which is most useful for its accuracy in placing and comfort of handling.

Mr. Norman Smith takes a great interest in fine heads which is certainly a fascinating hobby for the big-game hunter. There are many points in a head trophy to be considered. For instance, some people like length of horn, while others prefer weight and substance, and again many prefer width which shows up best on a wall. Here is a letter dealing with African buffalo heads :

" (13, Beaufort Gardens, S.W.3., Nov. 12th, 1927.)

" Thanks for yours. I thought the article would interest you if you saw it. The damage to the horn was repaired at Ward's so that you can't see it, and I presented the mounted head to the Conservative Club. I put my bullet to an inch, through the centre of the spine, and, of course, right through the lungs, the white stuff round the bullet hole being the lung froth, still bubbling out a few minutes after death. The ·475 was by Jeffery, and I used 'Dum-Dums,' with very small lead exposure. I prefer them for every shot at buffalo, except going straight away from you ; i.e. when following a wounded one. The spans though good, were nothing remarkable—43″ and 42¾″, but I saw none better. However, span isn't everything, and I regard the bosses of a buff as important as the mane of a lion. The 43″ head in my dining-room is one of the most perfect shaped buffalo heads I ever saw, in its prime, absolutely undamaged by fighting, etc., while the bosses rise in a high dome like a bee hive, ragged and gnarled, and come down over the forehead nearly to the eyes, the bosses also almost joining each other. It is a far handsomer head than most heads from 45″ to 47″.

"If ever you come to London let me know and come and see it and other heads. The 42¾″ head (in photo) with the disconsolate gunbearer on left of picture has flat and uninteresting bosses, and if his span had been 47″, I should have still given him to the Club and kept mine. I ought to have gone out there about 1912 and given myself two months at least, when I might have got a 50″, but no big span would satisfy me without first class bosses. Yes, I am very fit, seeing I am in my 63rd year. I enclose a spare print, rather a pale one I fear.

(Signed) "NORMAN B. SMITH."

"PS.—They omitted the following part of my article, which came at the end, perhaps for want of space :

"From what I have seen of buffalo in Kenya, and other parts of Africa, I am inclined to liberally discount many of the tales of their aggressiveness and ferocity, especially those of hunters being charged by whole herds. If this ever occurred no hunter, however expert, would live to tell the tale.

" Most of us find we have to keep our wits about us to stop a charge from a single animal, rarely though it should occur ; no one could stop more than two.

" If the gallant old rhino possessed the superior eyesight and cunning of the buffalo, he would, I think, be a more dangerous animal to hunt, as he has twice the pluck."

The foregoing letter gives a good idea of the chief points which constitute a really fine buffalo head, and I agree that fine bosses improve a head greatly and are more important than width, that is unless the span includes a proportionate thickness in the frontal horn.

Now follows a most interesting letter dealing again with small-bore rifles, the scenting powers of lions and methods of hunting these fine animals, and *herds* of buffaloes charging ! !

" (Clunes, Kirkhill, Inverness, Sept. 27th, 1928.)
" . . . I love my ·256 and my only reason for condemning such for use against dangerous game is that it increases the wounding, and above all the danger to other people, natives included, from wounded elephant, rhino, buffalo, and lion being about. Then again though I would certainly use

my ·256 on a lion if I had nothing larger, that is
because I have had enough experience to make me
expect to kill, but I would strongly urge a novice
not to try it. Many lions are poisoned in Kenya
nowadays, and a cattle owner is perhaps justified
in sitting up at night to kill the marauders.

" Somaliland was ideal for lion spooring. Hunting them with suitable dogs makes a certainty of
a large bag with very little risk. With a pack like
Rainey's, it is sheer murder. . . .

" I have no doubt lions make some use of scent,
when sniffing round a village, or cattle stockade,
etc. That they have anything approaching long
scent I don't believe, as I am sure you could creep
downwind to a lion without the least chance of
his scenting you at 100 yards or over, whereas
most African animals would certainly wind you at
300 yards.

" I am unable to believe that any animals can
wind a man so far as some book writers state.
E. G. ———— says an elk (Norway) can wind a
man three miles ! I like old ————, but he is too
dreadfully positive, even on subjects on which no
one can be certain.

" I feel sure that the chief reason that lions do
most of their hunting by night is because they can
see much better at night than their prey. Thus
owls and bats, which hunt at night and must be
able to see their prey. An owl will probably see
a mouse at night at a distance at which you and I
could hardly discern a cow.

" Amongst the nonsense I heard while in Kenya, when at Nairobi, was that buffalo were so aggressive that whole herds would sometimes charge, and —————— (a good talker through his hat, I think) had twice been charged by herds. No one would ever live to tell the story ! Again, when dining at Nairobi Club, one of the party asked me the measurement of the largest lion I had measured. I happen to have killed two exceptionally big ones, both with grand manes—one in Somali, 1896, one in Kenya, 1900. The latter had been seen and shot at at long range by a sportsman I met at Mombasa, who had been hunting on the Athi River, and got about six lions, none very good. He told me this was an enormous lion as he saw it several times, and as it was always with another lion with equally fine mane, and was far bigger than the latter, it must be exceptional. He said he fired at it at long range with a ·303, and thought he must have stung it as it grunted loudly.

" When I came across it out on the plain it was with the other, and I crawled to them, and got the big one running with my ·577/·500—the alarm being given by a jackal (waiting for a bit of the zebra they had killed) ; which winded me when the lions failed to do so. This fine lion measured 9 ft. 11 ins. on curve, and 9 ft. 8 ins. straight. When I gave the measures, a Major ——————, one of the party, and an assistant or honorary game warden of his district said : ' I wouldn't call that a big one. I saw two killed the same day 10 ft. 6 ins.

and 10 ft. 7 ins.' I said I thought that impossible as I didn't think many lions of 10 ft. or over had ever been killed. I proposed asking Leslie Tarlton, and his reply was that including what he had killed, and many killed by parties when he was acting as white hunter, he had been at the death of nearly 200, and had measured all the big ones, and the biggest straight measure was 9 ft. $8\frac{1}{2}$ ins. So much for the rot they talk. It was the same way with heads. I was asked to go and see and measure several heads of different species which were credited with big figures. All were considerably less. On the other hand, if so good a hunter and sportsman as Gilbert Blaine told me he had killed a wonderful measurement of any species, I should feel certain it was correct.

"I think one of the strongest points against lions having much scenting power is the fact that both Indian (in case of tigers) and Somali native shikaries never seem to think wind of importance in stalking them.

(Signed) " N. B. Smith."

In making references to above most interesting letter I need not discuss rifles as I have previously, in several places, given my opinion of them, and it is wholly a matter of preference founded on personal experience.

Regarding also the scenting powers of the felidæ I have expressed my views, but I very much doubt lions seeing much better at night than their prey, and the comparison between felines and owls does not strike me as being similar, for the following reasons.

Owls are practically blind in daylight and can hardly see their way about, especially if there is much glare, whereas lions, tigers and leopards can see quite well in the daytime. Antelopes sometimes rest at night, but can move about if they wish, and when attacked manage to keep clear of obstacles when they bolt.

As I have said before I believe the carnivora use their senses of smell and hearing as much as they do their powers of sight.

It is nonsense for people to say that herds of game, when they happen to run towards the hunter, ever charge *en masse*, and I agree with Norman Smith that such a statement is absurd. There was a lengthy controversy some years ago in the *Field* on this subject, as there has been on every other subject on big game, at one time or another. If a man happens to be in front of a herd of elephants or buffaloes which are rushing towards him, and the animals see him, they invariably split up and pass to either side, but it might easily happen, if the cover was thick, that they might miss doing so and knock the man over. If they did so they would probably get as much of a fright as would the human being, and in such a case, after doing so, would probably continue the retreat.

A hunter can tell at once whether an animal is frightened, suspicious, irritated or furious ; and with regard to the last two aspects neither are likely unless the animal has already been wounded by the hunter himself or by someone else before he came on it, so when we hear of *herds* of game

" charging " we can " take it with a very large grain of salt."

I quite agree with Mr. Smith that there is much rot talked about the habits and measurements of game by men who lack knowledge and observation. So long as it remains " talk " it is often amusing, but when it comes to making erroneous statements in the Press, or, worse still, in books, which have a longer life than newspapers, it is a pity. Thousands of people who have had no chance of big-game hunting but who enjoy reading about it are gulled, and they then proceed to gull others until totally wrong statements are disseminated to an ever-increasing circle. Some of us who believe in the truth try our best to correct misstatements about " twelve-foot " lions and tigers, elephant " cemeteries," " herds " of buffaloes " charging," and so on ; but it is almost a hopeless business to keep pace with those whose fulminations are manifestly fallacious. Another strange thing is that people who have had no experience of game will doubt some remarkable facts about them which are true, but will, on the other hand, believe the veriest nonsense which is utterly false.

In a recent letter dated January 31st, 1933, Mr. Norman Smith sent me a prescription for malarial fever which he assures me is an excellent remedy which might be useful to men who live in the tropics, so I have much pleasure in giving it here, for having been a malarious subject myself I am sorry I did not know about it when I lived in the African bush.

For Malaria

" On finding a temperature of 103° or more, indicating malaria, get into bed, and pile heaps of blankets on you. Then take one large tea spoon of Spirits of Nitre in a small tumbler of very hot water. This will very soon promote a profuse sweat, which must be allowed to continue for say half an hour while if any faintness occurs, as may happen in cases of extra high temperature such as 105°, take a sherry glass full of neat brandy of good quality. Then take off the blankets, rub down with a warm towel, and put on dry pyjamas, and one blanket to avoid chills.

" At no time take any quinine while a temperature exists. Next morning the temperature is almost certain to be normal, even though 105° the night before. Then take 5 grains quinine daily for two days, provided no temperature recurs ; then stop the quinine.

" In every case I have so far treated at the start of the malaria a complete cure has resulted in 48 hours. In one or two cases of long-standing malaria (say 3 weeks) and very high temperature, the cure has been complete in 3 days.

(Signed) " NORMAN B. SMITH."

These letters of Mr. Norman Smith interested me greatly, so I am sure others will also be glad to read them, for they contain exact knowledge on the subjects discussed. If some of them are controversial in a sense I think this is their best point, for controversy (so long as it is kept to fair comment) often brings out the truth on a subject, and the truth is all that matters, be the object big game or any other topic which interests human beings.

Fortunately the writer of these practical letters is still alive, and his views on shooting and natural history often appear over the word " Mannlicher " in the *Field*, and can be appreciated by those who take an interest in the same subjects. The risks he has run, especially when hunting lion, show that he possesses a cool head and a steady hand, both points of the utmost use to the hunter of dangerous game.

CHAPTER VI

Abel Chapman, Major C. E. Radclyffe, Charles Sheldon,
Major W. D. M. Bell, and Capt. J. Brander-Dunbar

MR. ABEL CHAPMAN was a voluminous writer on
large and small game, and he went for many trips
to various parts of the world, and never, I believe,
visited a country for sport without giving the
public a book worth reading. He was certainly a
good observer, and during his life took part in
many controversies.

Whether he was always correct in his views is
a matter of opinion, and according to individual
experience. I am one of those who believe in fair
controversy on matters about shooting and natural
history, because when doing so facts which have
escaped one's notice often crop up from the experience of others, which is sure to be different from
one's own.

Two men who hunt game, even in the same
country, have never come to the same conclusions.
The man who is oftenest right is the one with a
quick, logical brain and a keen eye for observation.

There are two important desiderata, and these
are : length of experience in a game country, either
by a long residence there, or by making many
trips to one district and concentrating on that

area. Many men can observe more in six months than another will do in six years; and because a man may have shot heaps of game it does not follow he knows more about their habits than an individual who has killed less.

Having read all of the late Abel Chapman's books, and many of his articles to the Press, I think his best volumes are those on sport and natural history in Britain and Europe, although his African books are also very interesting. His *Bird Life of the Borders* and *The Art of Wildfowling* will always be standard works on bird studies, and his *Wild Spain* and *Wild Norway*—the former written with Mr. Buck—are most excellent reading, but now very difficult to obtain.

Before I had the pleasure of meeting him we corresponded for some time, and here is one of his interesting letters :

" (Houxty, Wark-on-Tyne, Northumberland, 12/10/25.)

" I am now returning Stigand's book, which I have read, every page of it, with great pleasure. After one's small hunting days are over it delights to get back in imagination into those glorious wild regions of Africa, and to follow such a man as Stigand in his adventures.

" What a splendid fellow he was, but I never knew till I read his own account of it that he was the victim of that Lion incident at Simba. I remember it happening, and the semi-humorous description given in the Nairobi newspaper : *The*

Globe-Trotter, which I quoted in my *On Safari*
(p. 239), but without the slightest idea till now
that Stigand himself was the hero and the victim !
Curiously, last week I was shooting with Sir Alfred
Pease—his cousin Howard Pease of Otterburn
being a neighbour of mine—and we discovered
that he and I are also cousins in this way, that we
both descend from a 'joint' grandfather, whose
name was also Abel Chapman ! We had some
long yarns about the Athi, etc. The two cousins
were both shooting with poor George Grey, when
he was killed by a lion on Sir Alfred's estate on the
Athi Plains.

"Like yours, our shooting here is more hard
work than profit ! Game of all sorts is far too
scarce to 'drive,' so it's all 'padding the hoof,'
with about one shot per hour and a kill for every
two. Here is my home bag for September—
5 grouse, 8 blackcock, 26 partridge, 3 mallard,
2 teal, 6 snipe, 5 hares, and sundry sacksful of
bunnies ! Also seven salmon of from 8 lb. to
18 lb. The river is full of them now, but very
apathetic ! Well, my best thanks for the book. . . .
(Signed) " ABEL CHAPMAN."

Abel Chapman got some good salmon fishing
in his part of the Tyne which ran close to his house,
and he took a great interest in the stock of fish
which frequented his water. He sent me a letter
which begins with remarks on the prospects of
the breeding of the fish, and with an account of

the spawning habits of the salmon in the Tyne, and some remarks on a book he was reading on colour protection in animals. Like Selous, Stigand and others, he did not believe that the colour of animals, so far as it applies to the mammalia, could have the slightest effect in preserving them against their natural enemies. Certainly with insects, which live a quiescent life, colour may help, but not with mammals, as the animals which nocturnally prey on them hunt mainly by scent and hearing; and their sense of sight at night cannot be as strong as it is in daylight, although it is probably better far than human eyesight in the same conditions.

It must also be remembered that the animals which form the prey of the carnivora have equally good sight at night. Several times I have seen places where game had been attacked at night, and it was noticeable that when rushing away antelopes and zebras took care not to strike trees or rocks in their stampede towards safety. One has only to watch a cat hunting a mouse to see that the feline makes use of all its senses, and hearing most of all, as every now and again it stops to listen for the slightest movement made by its intended victim, so I fancy a lion, tiger or leopard acts in exactly the same way.

I know of cases, however, when smell was evidently the sense mainly used. For instance, lions attacked the mail-runners in Northern Rhodesia, so the men dropped their bags and bolted into the bush, and the animals immediately seized the bags, and mauled some of them badly, damaging many of the contents, including a letter to me from my mother. The post office people got a slip printed which they sent out with any letter which

A HUNTER'S HOME, LUAMBALI, N.E. RHODESIA

was marked, and I have still got it with the letter which is perforated by a lion's teeth. Here is a copy of the notice :

" The British South Africa Company,
    " Administration of North-Eastern Rhodesia,
        " Department of Posts and Telegraphs,
            " Postal Notice No. 8 of 1907.
                " MISSING MAILS
" It is hereby notified for general information that the carriers conveying the European and Colonial Mails, due to arrive at Fort Jameson on the 8th September, 1907, were attacked by lions near Mlilo's Village, Petauke Division, on the evening of the 2nd, and in consequence abandoned some of the bags and fired the grass.

" The mail bag despatched from Southampton on the 3rd August was partially destroyed by lions and by fire. The bag despatched from Salisbury on the 21st August, the bag despatched from Bulawayo on the 23rd August, one of the bags despatched from Livingstone on the 24th August, the Kalomo bag of the 24th August, and one bag from Broken Hill of the 26th August have not been recovered, and it is feared that they have been almost totally destroyed.

(Signed) " H. A. BALDOCK,
        " Comptroller of Posts and Telegraphs.
" General Post Office,
    " Fort Jameson,
        " 9th September, 1907."

Some day, I suppose, lions will become as extinct in Northern Rhodesia as are wolves in Britain, which will be a pity, for there is something exhilarating in living in a country where wild beasts still exist, and it adds a glamour to life to feel that civilization has not yet changed the primitiveness of conditions which have lasted for untold ages of time.

At the beginning of 1926 there was some controversy as to how African elephants got bits of stick or bamboo in their temple ducts, and a writer (who ought to have known better) suggested that the animals put them in themselves.

I took part in the correspondence, and finished it by suggesting that one might as well conceive the idea that they would pick their teeth, or scrape the mud off their feet on a log. I wrote to Abel Chapman and he replied in this letter :

" (Houxty, Wark-on-Tyne, 13/3/26.)

" Yes, it's very odd that elephants should collect sticks and twigs in their temple ducts—one might imagine that always pushing a way through impenetrable jungle, any ducts they have would be sure to get full of rubbish—but that's not a good enough reason for modern science, so, I suppose, they've to invent a better ? Also about ' scent ' ; I'm busy concocting a new article on ' Colour Protection,' which, incidentally, includes a survey of all the other protective senses—including ' smell,' and it surprises how little our great scientists recognise its strength and far-reaching range. I've got a few splendid passages on that !

" A thing that's taken my fancy in force is this :
That a recent expedition sent by the Union Government of South Africa into what used to be ' German
South-West Africa,' has sent in an official Report
which (though, of course, dealing in the main with
the grazing and agricultural aspects of the country,
its minerals, etc., etc.) also mentions incidentally
that the Faunal condition of the northern part
(adjoining Angola) remains in the same state of
primitive wealth of wild life as was the whole of
South Africa in the days of Gordon Cumming,
Harris, Baldwin, Oswell and the rest. Not only
do all the regular bigger beasts, from elephants
downwards, swarm, but they give reasons to believe
that the Quagga still exists there ! Also white
rhinos ! In solid fact there is no reason why they
shouldn't—for the Portugee (never a hunter) never
passed the Cunene river southwards, and the Dutch
always held to the north and east—never to the
westward, while the Germans (as usual) made a
hideous mess of their Colony, and then left it
severely alone. If only I wasn't so old (and so ill)
I'd start thither to-morrow. But alas, I can't throw
off the last of that congestion—only a trifling patch
remains, but it sticks worse than a limpet, and never
yet have I been out-of-doors. Bother ! When's it
to end ? When ?

(Signed) " ABEL CHAPMAN."

This letter is interesting, and regarding the state
of what was German-West, I remember meeting
an Army officer (British) on a voyage home who

had interests in that country, and had just come from the interior there. He mentioned the idea of the true quagga still existing there. However, as we met about 1907, and no word has come since of a quagga ever having been obtained there, the story must have been a myth, and I can imagine how it originated. For instance, a German, or a Dutchman, having heard the yarn that the quagga still existed may have seen some common Burchell's zebra at dusk with the light behind them, when they would look brown or black, and think they were quagga.

Zebras, when the light is thrown on them, look yellow or white coloured, but with the sun behind them seem to the hunter dark coloured. This, of course, only applies when they are some distance away, but the effects mentioned I have sometimes noticed when the sun was very strong at fifty or sixty yards.

I do not think Abel Chapman ever recovered from the illness he suffered. He still took a great interest in all matters regarding sport and natural history, and he, like others, objected strongly to the way scientists of the " dry as dust " order had of splitting up species on the grounds of slight variations which often occur.

A German Professor of Zoology once had the temerity to attempt a classification of the common, or Cape type of African buffalo, from the size and shape of their horns, forgetting that these trophies vary according to the age of the animals. The same applies to all horned game, such as the antelopes, goats or sheep, for in none of them does immature horn growth resemble the state attained in the full adult animals.

Here is a letter I got from Chapman on the subject :

" (Houxty, Wark-on-Tyne, 23/4/28.)

" Glad to hear from you again and that all goes well. I sent that note to the *Field* because I think it is utterly wrong, and dead against the true interest of zoological science to rush ahead with new Latin names the moment they get hold of a single specimen —or even a fragment of a single specimen. In the present case the second specimen annulled the whole claim of the first—but these cabinet-men of zoo and museum (who've never seen a wild beast in life) will stick to their Tom-fool tricks ! If you have *Savage Sudan* read the analogous cases of ' Mrs. Gray's Waterbuck ' at p. 160 et seq ; also the farce of ' Doratoceros triangularis ' two pages later, and there are scores of similar absurdities.

" I'm busy preparing a new sermon on that text !

" I escaped the winter by a really capital expedition to Egypt—most of the time spent among swarming wildfowl on Lake Menzaleh—800 square miles of it—and had many memorable experiences far too long to tell in a letter, and now we're back into mid-winter again—night frosts and snow every day—it has utterly ruined my April trouting that I look forward to all the year.

" Yes, I do know that mountainous road—beginning at St. Mary's, thence to Peebles, and on over the watershed to Moffat (nearly tumbling into the Devil's Beef-Tub on the way) !

"Kind remembrances to you both, and look in to see me if you are any way near.

(Signed) " ABEL CHAPMAN."

"PS.—Have just received a present of biltong from S. Africa—'rhino and giraffe'—hard as boards. Kindly meant, but not much use to a man without teeth! Like eating pit-props! It came from S.W. Africa—lately German."

This postscript is certainly amusing, for of all the meat one can tackle there is nothing harder or drier than African biltong, and I cannot imagine Chapman trying to masticate it.

His mention, too, of the Devil's Beef-Tub is interesting to me as I have passed it in a car dozens of times in all kinds of weather, from the sunny skies of summer to the icy blasts and blizzards of winter, making the road almost impassable with snow or a glassy covering of solid ice, where one has to "crawl" to be safe. Then at times one gets dense fogs which make the passage a slow business, unless one is to risk going "over the Khud," to use an Indian expression.

To show how fond Chapman was of his home and surroundings he wrote :

" (Houxty, 10/7/26.)

" No alas ! I wasn't at that Shikar Club dinner, didn't feel up to a 600 odd mile journey for a single evening's entertainment, besides, like you, I have no great inclination for social functions. I put

my name down as intending to be present if anyway
convenient, but am still on the feeble side after that
long illness, and never so happy as enjoying the
solitude of this terrestrial *Paradise* ! ! I can get
about a bit by car, and have been all around our
moors and lochs on this sheet of the ordnance map,
studying birds and beasts—even butterflies, and
that is a far greater joy than can be found in those
crowded cities ! Also I've resumed my fishing
as of yore, and done fairly well both with trout
and salmon. Of the latter have landed three this
week 6, 7½, and 8½ lbs., and hope to get another
to-night.

"No, I haven't seen Sir T. Cook's *Sunlit Hours*—
in fact had not even heard of it so must try to get
a look at it. Percival's East African book is splendid. I knew him well in Kenya—a splendid hunter,
but never suspected such literary abilities to lie in
his breast.

"I also knew Brander-Dunbar, and was at
Pitgaveny several years ago—found a pair of black-
tailed Godwits nesting on Loch Spiney—never
before known to do so in Scotland ! ['Spiney'
should be Spynie.—D.D.L.]

"Grouse prospects here (by report of keepers
and shepherds) bad, but I'm not quite inclined to
accept their verdict always. Fear I won't get so
far as Peebles this summer, or will certainly call
and see you.

"With kindest remembrances to you both.

(Signed) "ABEL CHAPMAN."

The next letter was on the old subject of the hunting habits of the carnivora and it is worth giving :

" (Houxty, Wark-on-Tyne, 12/7/28.)

" Oh yes ! That new book of mine is causing a flutteration in many dovecots—especially re ' Colour Protection,' and the hunting habits of the big felines. It's been rather amusing. A lot of Indian shikaris (first-rate sportsmen, I doubt not) started a red-herring drag in *The Times* that in India tigers hunt habitually by sight and in daylight, and don't use their noses at all. Well, it may be so —I've not been in India so won't deny it—all the same I won't believe a word of it, and the evidence they bring forward in support of their contention is almost puerile. At first I made up my mind not to reply, but they asked me to do so—so you will find a long screed in to-day's *Times* (11th). I wish you would read it ! ' Colour Protection,' too, I've treated in the book in terms that leave nothing more to be said. I wish you had it, but have so much in stake in it, can't afford to give 'em away ! Lots of my critics haven't read the book, but pick out some sentence from the reviews —wrench it from its context—frame it in a totally different environment—and then say it's wrong ! Well, I just haven't time to reply to all that sort of ' poop,' so let it slide and they stew in their own juice.

" I'm sorry to say there are grave doubts about

the grouse locally. One keeper (on 11,000 acres)
tells me the bulk of the young broods have been
drowned, but I rather doubt that without further
evidence, and imagine he is a bit of a pessimist,
anyway on other moors it certainly isn't nearly so
bad as that, although there has been a regrettable
degree of mortality through the cold and incessantly
wet weather. We can't even get a proper share
of the salmon when one flood follows on the heels
of another.

" Oh, the correspondence this new book entails !
I seem to spend half each day quill-driving ! So
forgive a rather hasty scrawl.

(Signed) " ABEL CHAPMAN."

Once one begins a controversy, Abel Chapman
probably found like others, there is no end to
criticism, as it is apt to wander from the objective
at issue.

I have known a correspondence on the habits of
tsetse flies develop into the feeding propensities of
lions ! ! !

Here is a rather amusing epistle :

" (Houxty, Wark-on-Tyne, Northumberland,
    26/7/28.)

"Lions ! Yes the Editor of The Shooting Times
kindly sent me the paper with yet more criticisms,
but I don't feel equal to engaging in another newspaper controversy. Fact is, age begins to tell,
and one has ups and downs. Some mornings I

can spring out of bed keen as a steel rat-trap, others one feels like a bit of boiled string—or a worm ! And of late I've rather been in the latter wretched condition, besides I've really said already (in my book and in the *Times* letter) all I know on the subject that's worth saying. These critics in the ' S.T.' keep on harping on India, where I've never been—and tigers which I've never seen—also panthers which I don't know what they are unless it's an alias for leopard ?

" Then about Colour Protection—that chapter in *Retrospect* was merely the sequel to a far more elaborate essay on the subject in *Savage Sudan,* and in it are set-out, with the utmost care the axioms, the rules, and the exceptions. If critics (as is only fair) would first read that, they would find all their arguments met beforehand—in short they are simply beating the empty air, and I can't go over it all again. It's a case of ' arguing for argument's sake,' and if they really want to understand they should begin by learning the A.B.C. of the subject and not start at the X.Y.Z. ! ! ! Your examples, I am sure, are all excellent and to the point in both cases, but oh ! what a lot of writing it would involve ! Really the two subjects would require a whole volume apiece !

" Alas ! that poor airman on ' Broadlaw.' I know almost the very spot where he struck—and no wonder when the tops were all shrouded in thick fog. I've wandered all over those wild hills and love them, but they're too big now ! "

I got many letters from Abel Chapman, and have only given a few of the number. He usually ended up with " Yours ever," and his was a lovable character ; in fact a " dear old fellow " is the expression several of his friends used when speaking of him.

There is a society of big-game hunters in Britain known as the Shikar Club, which was founded in the early part of this century by Capt. (now Major) C. R. E. Radclyffe, who wrote that excellent book on American hunting, *Big-Game Shooting in Alaska*, published by Rowland Ward, Ltd., in 1904.

About that time, when I was hunting in Nyasaland and N.E. Rhodesia, Capt. Stigand and myself each got a letter from Mr. J. E. Harting of the *Field* asking us if we would like to join, and we both did so.

The chairman of the club is the well-known sportsman Lord Lonsdale, and both he and Major Radclyffe have, since the club was founded, spent much effort and money in keeping it going, and so far as I know received little if any thanks for doing so.

At the annual dinner arranged on Oaks night members meet and discuss matters connected with big game, and anyone who proposes to go a trip to some region where he has not shot in before is sure to meet a fellow-member who can " put him wise " about conditions. If such a member is not there his address can be found in the list of members published every year. Many of the most prominent members have passed on to other " happy hunting grounds," such as Selous, George Grey, St. George Littledale, J. G. Millais, Abel

Chapman and others, and when one compares an early list with the one printed this year many of the names are new. Although the writer is not an original member, he was elected a few months after the formation of the club.

Needless to remark, the members are good sportsmen who have shot in most places of the world where big game exists. The damage they do to the game is nothing compared to those who kill for meat or hides, for their purpose is to obtain good trophies, and this means that only the best males are shot. I think it is a pity that some such club is not started in important centres in India and Africa, as anything which will foster sportsmanlike methods will naturally tend to the further preservation of the game throughout the world.

Here is a letter I received from Major C. E. Radclyffe in which he says something about the prospects of big game :

" (Hyde, Wareham, 8th August, 1911.)

" Many thanks for your letter of July 1st re shooting in Nyasaland, which I am keeping to show to any member of our Club who may think of visiting that country.

" Some time ago I had a number of letters from a Mr. Harger who was living at Blantyre, and as they were very interesting in the way he dealt with the subject of game and the tsetse fly, I published them all in the *Field*, and this stirred up a great controversy on the subject.

" I fear from what I can hear, that there will

soon be an agitation throughout most of Africa for the destruction of the game. And then perhaps after they have killed off a valuable asset, the residents will find they have still got the flies wherever they keep domestic cattle.

" I cannot myself see any reason why if the fly follow a herd of buffalo, that they will not also follow domestic cattle.

" I am leaving England in a few days for a long trip in North America. That is a country where people have awakened to the value of the big game, and where they are now taking wise steps to protect it.

(Signed) " C. E. RADCLYFFE."

The remarks about the U.S.A. taking steps to preserve the remaining game are interesting. Had it not been for men like Mr. Charles Sheldon, Mr. G. L. Harrison and others, they would soon have been too late. They almost exterminated the bison (called " buffalo "), wapiti and prong-horned antelope, and this was mainly due to skin and meat hunters.

The wapiti (called " elk ") were actually shot down largely for their teeth, to supply the members of " Elk Clubs "—whatever that may mean. I have read that the teeth of wapiti get a golden metallic colouring which started this absurdity. Such a craze, one would imagine, is more fitted for a children's game than an aspiration in adults. How can a wapiti's tooth, an elephant-hair bangle or a hare's foot affect human affairs, and white people who believe in such nonsense are worse than the witch doctor who carried a charm which he thought would deflect high-velocity bullets and " turn them to water."

In Africa many natives carry a charm ; it may be a seed, a chip of stone, or made up of some concoction got from animal or vegetable matter.

Before starting out for the first hunt of a season the native trackers will have a dance round the weapon, and perform strange rites over and around it. They do not believe the firer has much to do with its powers to hit or kill. These remain in the weapon itself, so unless it is propitiated it will act wrongly when it is brought into action.

They have many other weird beliefs, one of the queerest being about elephant tusks. When an elephant has been killed and cut up, the tusks, after being removed, are taken away into a hidden place and the nerve matter removed. They think that if a young person of either sex sees this done he or she will become infertile. It is always an old man who performs this operation in secret, and he keeps off any young unmarried person who happens to come near him. This is usually accompanied by such a lurid description of the results of observing the ceremony that the youngster bolts as if a leopard were chasing behind !

White people, too, are subject to beliefs which hardly seem rational. For instance, a person may say " Touch wood " to divert bad luck, which, of course, is pure nonsense.

But to return to my letters, I would like to give a very interesting one from that fine hunter and field-naturalist, the late Charles Sheldon, who wrote several most charming books on American

big game and natural history, the best being one
entitled *The Wilderness of Denali*, which was published in 1930, after his death.

He was a very hardy hunter and a wonderful
observer of the habits of American game, and a
close friend was Selous, whom he once accompanied
on a trip into Yukon territory.

I wrote him about the rifles he preferred and here
is his reply :

" (3022 P. Street, Washington, D.C., Jan. 13th,
      1928.)

"I was glad indeed to receive your letter, and
hear of your admiration for Selous. I share your
feeling completely, and have preserved all his
letters to me extending over several years. Aside
from admiration his character and personality was
one which got into a fellow's heart. My association
with him keeps alive vivid memories which will
endure as long as I shall live.

" Only a few weeks ago I was dining with Willie
Moncrieffe, 'W.M.' of Selous's book, *Sport and
Travel*, page 148. He had much to say on Selous,
but what interested me particularly was the fact
that of all sportsmen who had, during Moncrieffe's
experience of many years, visited that region,
Selous, who had never hunted Wapiti before, was
the only one whom the guides followed, rather than
led, during the hunt.

"You ask me about a comparison of rifles—
my ·256 as compared with modern ' magnums.'

I regret that I have had no experience either with 'magnums,' or with game outside this continent.

"Before 1899 I was living in Mexico where game was abundant at the time, deer, antelope, grizzly bears, and mountain sheep. I used at first a ·303 Mannlicher, the bullets heavily tipped with lead. Since they too often passed entirely through antelope, deer and sheep, tearing a large surface on emergence I purchased from Jeffery's in London a ·256 rifle. I have used this same rifle continuously and exclusively, and will continue to use it I hope for many more years. The first bullets were the Jeffery split ones. Though occasionally one would shatter yet they were satisfactory. But when your book *Central African Game* was published in 1906, I sent and obtained the bullets recommended and have used them exclusively ever since. They have been completely satisfactory, not one ever having shattered, always penetrating the animal to a vital point from any angle.

"I have at 200 yards hit both moose and grizzly bears in the stern, the bullet breaking the hip and penetrating to the lungs and heart, well mushroomed but whole.

"It seems to me perfectly clear that the ·256 with the right bullet at a muzzle velocity of 2300 ft. is completely satisfactory for all game on this continent, including moose, caribou and large bears, many of which I have killed during years of hunting them. My experience to me is a demonstration that with ·256 it is only a question of directing the bullet at a vital or disabling spot.

" I have taken the liberty of sending your letter to my friend Elton Clark of Boston who has taken great interest in rifles, and has hunted much in this country and some in Africa. He seeks what he believes is perfection in rifles, and has tried many rifles, though I doubt if he has tried less than ·275. I hope that you may hear from him.

" Since I have always hunted alone I have not even had the experience of observing the results of rifles of others.

" For some years I have been hunting the mountain sheep of the deserts of the South-West, tracing them from the Colorado River south to their southern range in the Gulf of California in Sonora, Mexico, and in Lower California. Along with them I get deer and a few antelopes. There is little difficulty of killing them with any modern rifle.

" I have published no other books than those mentioned by you, though I have several manuscripts which I have never offered to a publisher. Perhaps the constant ' ego ' of a lone hunter describing his experiences has been a cause of hesitation further to exploit it. I published an unimportant article along with the last Boone and Crocket Club book and wrote the appendix A adopted by the club. The whole book has other chapters of some interest and I shall take pleasure in asking the publishers to send you a copy. All your books including the last one are in my library read and re-read.

" A few evenings ago I saw good motion pictures of an African hunt, the motor cars replacing the Safari. In Alaska now airplanes take one to the hunting country in a few hours to points where weeks of toil were required to reach when I hunted there. The hunter wires the airplane to go in and establish the camp in the hunting ground. He reaches the point of departure on the coast, and the next morning, after a few hours' flight he can kill game. Before long the whole wilderness in this continent will resound with the steam whistle, the noise of the motor, and the buzz of the airplane. I rejoice that I have had my share of the enjoyment of primitive wilds, and of the vicissitudes of reaching them. I should imagine that Africa is rapidly reaching the same state.

" This letter has rambled on at length for I was so glad to hear from you.

(Signed) " C. SHELDON."

This splendid hunter and field-naturalist died in Nova Scotia on September 21st, 1928.

He took a great interest in game preservation in the United States of America, and the formation of the great Mount McKinley National Park was largely due to his efforts. Most of his hunting was done in the interest of natural-history research, and he was moderate always. He saw that if something was not quickly done to preserve the fauna it would soon be exterminated, which proves that the best hunters are the best preservers of the natural life of a country.

His remarks on the bullets he used in his ·256 are interesting, and how, after trying several types, he found the " Dum-Dum " the best for reliability. Of course, it is impossible to get any certain type of bullet to act the same in a variety of animals which differ in size. For instance, a "Dum-Dum " will go through all antelopes up to the size of reed-buck and bushbuck with side shots, but in roan and sable antelopes, if they hit the shoulder-bone, they may stay inside. For a collector a bullet which expands and makes an exit hole as big as an orange naturally spoils the skin badly for mounting; in fact, it would be necessary to put on a patch of skin to cover the hole and this would show as an unsightly mark.

Sheldon's comments about the way the wilderness in North America is being opened up by the use of aeroplanes also applies, I suppose, to Africa, and it was inevitable that such an invention would soon make a great difference in conditions. I agree with him that the old days were more interesting, when a man spent some time in getting to the hunting ground. For example, in tropical Africa one would tramp along with the carriers, doing from twenty to twenty-five miles a day foot-slogging. This made one hard, so when the shooting country was reached the hunter was in good form and fit for the most strenuous work. This would not apply to a man who sits in an aeroplane, or a motor car, nor would he feel the long-drawn-out fascination of the slower foot journey, with all the vicissitudes and difficulties which had to be overcome. In Africa I even hated to use a *machilla* (hammock on one or two poles carried by natives), as it seemed a lazy way of getting about and it made one soft and flabby. The only good it seemed to do for those who had a sluggish liver was to stir it up. It did this so much to some people that the wobbling made them violently sick.

Those who have lived into this wonderful age of mechanical development, and had the opportunities of trying the various methods of travel, almost invariably prefer the older ways, for they added a glamour and romance which the new-fangled systems lack. Moreover, the old ways were more beneficial to the natural fauna of the world and led to less persecution and disturbance.

Sheldon was a man, like a few others, including myself, who liked the lonely methods of hunting, when one is not distracted by worries caused by others, and has a better chance of making observations. Only once did I join a party, and that was enough for me, as it was not a pleasant party ! It is an extraordinary thing that men who can get on well in civilized conditions, where there are comforts, immediately get irritable under the stress of hard travel and quarrel about the merest trifles. Therefore, a man will almost always be happier when he is alone on a hunting trip, except for his white or black employees, which will be necessary wherever he goes. Here again natives will prove more obedient than whites, so the best places to hunt in are in countries where native labour is procurable.

All people who have shot in Africa have heard of Major W. D. M. Bell, who has probably killed more African elephants than anyone else, but is so modest about his doings that nobody has yet discovered the exact figures.

We have corresponded about rifles, and as he has given me permission to use his interesting letters, I gladly do so, for he is the greatest exponent of the small bore I know of, so what he has to say on the subject should interest others. Here is his first letter to me :

" (Corriemoillie, Garve, Ross-shire, 8/12/1924.)

" Many thanks for your letter. I did not answer it sooner as I only got it on my return here.

"What perfect nonsense they are writing in ——— about it being non-sporting to use a small bore for big game. The idea, I suppose, that it would lead to wounding. As we know this is not so when the small bore is in the hands of an expert. An expert small bore shot at heavy game becomes so as the result of experience. The novice must start somewhere, so let him begin with the weapon which feels best to him for the job, I say. The ordinary average city man, out for rhino say, will undoubtedly feel better about it when carrying a double ·470 or ·577 than he would with a ·256 or ·275. We must not forget that he has not had the opportunities that we have had of knocking rhino spinning with a ·256. Therefore I take it the novice is behaving in a more sportsmanlike way when he arms himself with the deadliest weapon he can obtain, i.e. a heavy double.

" For anyone to say that because one uses a

small bore to kill big game with, that therefore he is not a sportsman is simple nonsense, and is not worth arguing with, provided always that the user of the small bore prefers it as the result of his own experience.

(Signed) " W. D. M. BELL."

The foregoing is just my idea, for, as I have said before, " let a man use what he prefers." Then follows an interesting letter on experiments with different rifles :

" (Corriemoillie, Garve, Ross-shire, 8th February, 1933.)

" DEAR LYELL,

" Thank you very much for your letter, so sorry for delay in answering it : I have been mixing it with the ' flu.'

" I feel very much flattered by your suggestion of including my paltry letter in your forthcoming book, and I will send you a snap-shot in a few days.

" I still use the ·275, and your penetrating surmise that I use the ' Magnum ' for stags is correct.

" While on the subject of rifles I was wondering if you have ever done any investigating into the course of bullets through various substances. I have been doing so recently and some curious things have come up.

" Of course it is impossible to reproduce artificially the exact conditions a bullet encounters in an elephant's head, for instance. But for the purpose of my experiments I chose a series of layers of Scotch oak, sapwood, and heartwood. The latter is, as you know, extremely dense, tough and hard. Behind the target I placed a box of sawdust about 4 ft. square.

" You would hardly believe it, unless you have tried it, but a great many of the bullets escaped the box altogether, although it was placed immediately behind the target.

" Several bullets were so deflected as to strike 7 ft. from the straight line of flight in a horizontal distance from the target of 10 ft.

" The worst offenders in this respect were the short dumpy so-called ' Big Game ' type.

" A very fine performance was put up by the ·318 bullet of 250 grains. But even here the deflection caused by firing at the target from a slight angle was fantastic, so much so as to miss the catching box entirely.

" The pointed H.V. bullets were, of course, quite hopeless.

" It seemed to be that the most reliable bullet for holding a true course through layers of varying density were those having as characteristics (what a word !), long body, weight and long straight sides, as opposed to short body, weight and sloping sides.

" If I were designing a bullet for the killing of large animals I would take a calibre of about ·300. Anything smaller than this diameter would tend to bend, as does the ·256, an otherwise very good performer.

" If pressures would allow of a weight of 250 grains, that, or as near it as possible would be my aim. Then I would try to drive it with a slow-burning powder, as used in the German Halger, as near to 2600 ft. p.s. as possible, and if under these conditions the envelope showed signs of rupturing, or flattening at the nose I would strengthen it.

" The best bag I ever made in one day was when using a ·318. I had 35 cartridges with me, and I killed 19 bulls. I had 8 misfires, and two or three left over at the end. It was in the days when the case was escaping the striker through having defective shoulder. They have overcome this diffi-culty now, at any rate I had no misfires when I was experimenting recently. But I would like to see a belt on this case, or better still an enlarged powder space.

"I have just been reading ———. I gather the author is ratty about small bores for big stuff ; at any rate I notice one or two rather sarcastic references to myself in this regard. What is it that seems to heat them up so ? It must be some inner consciousness of inferiority I think. At any rate I never had any elephant I had shot at carried off the field by his pals, as the author says occurred to him.

" What sustains the big bore men is the thought that weight of metal will cover deficient accuracy, allowing them another chance to blot the fellow out, and they should admit it, instead of trying to make out that it is not ' sporting ' to use small bores.

" Would it be ' sporting ' to use a field gun ?

" Are you ever up in these parts ? I would very much like to meet you and have a yarn over old days.

" Yours sincerely,
(Signed) " W. D. M. BELL."

In reply to above interesting letter recording the writer's experiments with different rifles and projectiles I suggested the deflection at times was caused by knots and hard patches in the wood, in which he agrees.

In his interesting book, *The Wanderings of an Elephant Hunter*, Major Bell mentions that the elephant which bore the heaviest tusk known, which is in the Natural History Museum at South Kensington, was shot by a native with an old muzzle-loader on the slopes of Mount Kilimanjaro. The tusk weighs 226½ lbs., is 10 ft. 2½ ins. long on outside curve, and the girth 24¼ ins.

It probably was the tusk often referred to which weighed, when brought to London, 235 lbs., and lost in drying 8½ lbs., as all tusks decrease slightly in weight after a few years.

When in Zanzibar, about the year 1907, I bought an enlargement of two enormous tusks, one of which is certainly the one in the Natural History Museum. It has for some time been a mystery where the other tusk was which many supposed to be a pair. Anyone knowing anything about ivory can see in the photograph that though the tusks are a right and left they are not from the same elephant, as their lengths and curves differ considerably.

In *East Africa* of March 16th, 1933, appeared a letter by Mr. V. Myers saying his firm are the owners of this tusk, so I wrote to him to ask for its full description, and whether he agreed with my supposition that the tusks in the Zanzibar photograph of two natives holding them against a carved Arab door were not a pair from the same elephant. I received this reply:

" (15 to 20 Tower Hill, London, E.C.3, 17th March, 1933.)

" I am obliged for your letter of the 16th, which I find most interesting. The tusk you mention is the one in question, and although it has always been described as forming a pair to the one in the Natural History Museum, it is not, as you surmise, the fellow tusk.

" I am of the same opinion as you that both these tusks have shrunk in weight on account of drying.

" The one that we have weighs 214 lbs., and the length including curve is 10 ft. 5½ ins., length of hollow part 29¼ ins. The girth at the hollow end, 3 ins. from end of the tusk, is 23 ins.

" If you would care to see this tusk, it is at present lying with Messrs. Rowland Ward Ltd., ' The Jungle,' 167, Piccadilly, W.1, although it is still our property.

" I am not quite sure whether I have your book

The African Elephant and its Hunters amongst my collection of works on Elephant and Ivory, but I shall look through my library to-night, and if it is not in my possession I think I should like to have it. I will let you know. Perhaps you can tell me also whether your book can be purchased?

" If at any time you are in London, I shall be delighted to see you.

" The *Public Ledger* is shortly putting in an article on Ivory in connection with our firm, and I will send you a copy.

(Signed) " V. MYERS."

This is extremely interesting, as I have now found out where the second great tusk is, for I do not know how many times I have seen the Zanzibar photograph referred to as if they were a true pair —that is, two tusks from the same elephant.

It has always amused me to think that the finest tusker which there is any record of was shot by an unwashed savage, when many white hunters would have given anything to have obtained such a prize. Here was a native using an old muzzle-loader, probably a flint-lock, who had the luck to get him, when there were Europeans in the country who possessed the best of rifles and cartridges who given the chance, would have bagged him. The longer one lives the more does one realize that Providence, Fate, Luck, or whatever one may call it, is a "will-o'-the-wisp," which scatters fortune in the most promiscuous manner, and it is impossible for humans to do more than try their best to succeed in anything they undertake. The rest is chance !

The finest tusker shot by a European is one shot in the Congo by Major P. H. G. Powell-Cotton which had tusks of 198 and 174 lbs.—the heavier being 9 ft. on outside curve and 25 ins. in circumference.

In the Lonsdale Library volume, *Big-Game Shooting in Africa*, edited by Major H. C. Maydon, the lucky sportsman gives an interesting account of how he killed this splendid elephant.

In his interesting letter Major Bell makes some justifiable remarks about those who criticize the users of small-bore rifles and say it is not " sporting " to use them. I agree with him that those who do this probably suffer from an " inner consciousness of inferiority," for it has been proved hundreds of times that a cool, steady shot can do better work with an accurate ·256 or ·275 than he can with a ·470 or ·577.

Certainly let those who believe in the big bore use one if it gives them confidence, but also let them remember that those who trust in the small bore do so because they found them handier and more accurate, and that they did better work with them. It is noticeable that the more expert a man is the more does he favour the small bullet, and Bell is the most prominent example of this among African elephant hunters.

For many years I have known Capt. James Brander-Dunbar, of Pitgaveny, Elginshire, and when living at " The Camp," in Zomba, Nyasaland, in 1903, I remember him arriving there on a shooting trip to his old haunts, as he had previously been attached to the King's African Rifles in that Protectorate. He certainly livened up " The Camp " when he was preparing his *ulendo* (trip), and I have a vivid recollection of a wrestling encounter between him and Capt. C. H. Stigand in the billiard-room of the mess which lasted for some time.

Stigand was well over six feet, and very powerful, and I believe that, when he was being coached for the Army, Sandow told him that he could train him into being the strongest man in the world, which, of course, was a problematical prediction!

Brander-Dunbar was much shorter in stature, but he made up for it by being exceptionally muscular and tough. I think the friendly combat ended by both of them rolling under the billiard-table when a game was proceeding. They shifted the table, and a spirit-level had to be found to test it, which put an end to one of the most amusing wrestling matches I have ever witnessed!

Brander-Dunbar has written me many letters on African game and other subjects. He is an excellent shot with rifle and scatter-gun, and his knowledge of the African fauna is great, as he has shot in much wild country, when game was more plentiful and conditions more favourable than they are to-day. In one letter he says : " I have had a pretty wide experience of all the dangerous beasts existing from the North to South Africa.

" I cannot exactly say how many elephants and buffaloes I have killed, but of lions I have killed a few, though I never particularly looked for them as the fewer shots fired when in elephant country the better."

He thinks the leopard is a good deal more coura-geous than the average lion when wounded, and there is no doubt that this is so, for I am sure had as many leopards fallen to rifles as have lions there would be a greater average of charges. In Africa for every leopard that is killed in fair hunting probably ten or more lions have been " bagged." A leopard is one of the quickest creatures in existence, and his movements are so rapid that when he is in a hurry all one sees is a streak of yellow. For a wounded leopard there could not be a better weapon to use than a shotgun with S.S.G. or A.A.A. pellets— that is, at close range.

In the old days Brander-Dunbar used a double oval-bore loaded with 9 drams of black powder. He tells me it left a copious blood spoor, which is always useful if an animal struggles off in thick bush. The greatest fault of small-bore H.V. rifles is the small amount of blood left behind by a stricken beast. He likes the Ross ·280 rifle, which, however, sometimes displays the bad fault of failing to extract the fired case.

Brander-Dunbar, like all experienced men, believes in getting to close quarters, and though to the novice this seems very dangerous, it is much less so than firing at long range and then having to follow up. Animals seldom think of charging until they are hurt, and with elephants one should get to within twenty to thirty yards before firing the first shot.

In a letter Brander-Dunbar mentions how often there is the greatest difficulty in reaching a vital spot in an elephant, and particularly is this difficult with the head shot. This is caused, I imagine, by the condyle, or protuberance of the lower jaw, intervening, and the closer one is the greater the difficulty of reaching the brain with the side shot. Therefore, for head shots from the side, a distance of forty yards would be better than one of ten paces, as then there would be a lesser chance of

J. BRANDER–DUNBAR

R. J. CUNINGHAME

the bullet being deflected.   Modern H.V. nickel
or steel-covered projectiles are much more liable
to go astray on knobs of bone than were the old
lead bullets, because the former are so much harder.
A leaden bullet would glance, too, on occasion,
but would not do so as readily, for it would dent
considerably and still keep a true course.

Here is a fine account of following a wounded
bull buffalo from a letter of Brander-Dunbar's :

" I once had to follow a wounded bull through
swampy ground covered with a breast high iris-
like growth, and clumps of half-burned tenka-
tenka every few yards.   I was leading on the blood
spoor when it became evident that we were very
close to our quarry.   Although the men trusted
me absolutely there was considerable hesitation
when I suggested, in order to allow me free to
look out for squalls, that an unarmed tracker should
take the lead.   We had hardly changed places
when the buff's head appeared through the tenka-
tenka at right angles to his tracks.   At this duelling
range he simply sank into grass with a bullet in his
brain."

When following wounded dangerous game in
thick cover a tracker should always be in front
doing the spooring, with the European close behind,
so that he can be looking ahead and around, for no
one can track and do this at the same time.   As
soon as the animal is seen the tracker should sink

down so as not to impede the shot. Should an animal get to close quarters a native will seldom be caught, for they can run and jink like wild pigs, and climb like monkeys !

I have seen Brander-Dunbar, round Duffus Castle, pulling down geese from the sky with a Magnum 12-bore pump-gun in a most satisfactory manner, and on his Loch Spynie—a wonderful haunt of ducks and wildfowl—the trout fishing used to be most excellent. He had an old curly retriever dog which used to retrieve fish from the water when hooked without damaging them in the slightest degree.

When staying in Elginshire I was keen to see the trophies in his kinsman's house, Altyre, particularly the wonderful white rhino horns, so he obtained permission from Sir A. P. Gordon Cumming, Bt., for me to do so, and we motored there one day. The larger horn, measuring $62\frac{1}{4}$ ins. on front curve, is a most remarkable trophy, and Roualeyn Gordon Cumming, who brought it home, so far as I can discover in his book *A Hunter's Life in Africa*, does not say whether he shot the animal or traded the horn. He may have killed it, but if so it is strange he does not mention the fact in his well-known work.

The entrance-hall in Altyre is the finest of the kind I have seen, and it is crammed with trophies of the chase, curios, and weapons, including old guns, rifles, swords and daggers, with some family portraits. The surroundings of wild country are in keeping with the beauty of the house, and it is a home to be appreciated, but the ruinous taxation of the present age must " take the gilt off the ginger-bread," to use a slang term.

Roualeyn Gordon Cumming has been accused

of slaughtering game, but it must be remembered that when he shot in Southern Africa no one ever thought that all the killing that took place could make much difference. The chief exterminators were certainly the Boers, who hunted for meat and skins, for men like Gordon Cumming were only in the country for a limited period. Moreover, they were accompanied by such a horde of natives that I doubt if much of the meat was wasted.

These old nimrods must have been extremely tough and vigorous men, for carrying their heavy and unwieldy weapons, and loading them on horseback, must indeed have been strenuous work. They must often have returned to camp exhausted by their great exertions in the hunting field and it was only the strongest who could stand the life for long.

CHAPTER VII

Lecture given by R. J. Cuninghame, M.C., entitled
" The Story of the Elephant "
(New Galloway, March 4th, 1921)

IT is my privilege this evening to read to you a paper on the subject of elephants, and I think it may be just as well if we make a start from the very early times in order to trace, ever so briefly, the ancestors of our present elephant.

These elephants of ours are the largest terrestrial mammals at present existing, though it is not the largest of mammals in the world. This honour is held by the whale, who measures some 70 to 80 feet in length, and, as a wood merchant might say, weighs about one ton to the running foot.

The elephant scales only about five or six tons, but he is representative of the largest of present-day proboscideans. Now please do not think I am going to cram a lot of long scientific names into this paper. There will be only three or four altogether. We will leave them for scientific occasions, and endeavour, as far as possible, to call a spade a spade, and not some name of ten syllables, composed of Latin and Greek, with perhaps a dash of Hebrew in it to make it taste pleasant when you have got to say it, but, sad to relate, I have never

yet come across one of these long names that had a
wee taste Scotch in it.

The name " proboscideans " comes from two
Greek words meaning " to feed before."

Such a long time ago, that you may call it a few
million years, more or less, and it won't make any
difference, there were some small mammals about
the size and shape of the present-day American
tapir.

I am afraid I must give the scientific names of
just three of the most pronounced types of the
prehistoric progenitors of our modern elephant,
as unfortunately they do not possess any other
names. But for simplicity's sake I will refer to
them as Forms 1, 2 and 3.

As far as scientists have established, the first of
all the elephants rather resembled the present-day
South American tapir. We will refer to him
as Form 1, but his real name is Metherium, which
means the beast with the movable snout, and its
remains are found in a very early geological period
called the Lower Eocene.

He was rather a pig-like animal, with a very
movable snout of some four or five inches long.
The eye was small and placed very much forward
in the head, near to the corner of the mouth.   There
were two small canine teeth in the upper jaw,
and two incisors or front teeth about three inches
long protruding in a downward curve exactly
like those of the present-day walrus. In the lower
jaw there were only two front teeth, and they stuck
straight out in front of the jaw about two inches.
Every foot carried four distinct toes, and the body
was probably well covered with hair.

This little animal was the father of all future

forms of elephants, and he lived just before the time when the coal we burn to-day was being formed. To allow you some conception of the remoteness of the period referred to, I may mention that it requires about one million years to form one inch in depth of coal in a coal seam. Some seams are, say, twenty-five feet in thickness, and the fossil remains of the little pig-like Metherium are found underneath the first one-inch of coal. Now you will see why I told you that a few million years, more or less, in time estimation, really matters very little.

Well, as time passed slowly on and the pig with the snout had ceased to exist, there appeared another animal related to him, and we will refer to him as Form 2.

His name is the Paleo Mastodon, or ancient toothed animal, and he is found in the Eocene period. In size he was about three times as big as Form 1, and the eye was placed in much the same part of the head as in our modern elephant. The snout was twice the length of Form 1, and readily prehensile—in fact, it was a real elephant's trunk in miniature. Both the two upper tusks of Form 1 have disappeared, but the two lower front teeth remain about the same size, only more substantial. The two upper front teeth are still curved like a walrus, but very much longer and stouter than in Form 1. The ear was set lower and more flattened out against the side of the head, and the whole skull had assumed a long, wedge-shaped appearance, quite different to the somewhat rabbit-shaped skull of Form 1.

Form 3 was called Tetrabelodon, and this fellow is the last I shall trouble you about. The long

name means the animal with four tusks to fight
with, and he flourished during the Miocene period,
which was a mighty long time after the Eocene.

In all respects of size and shape this Form 3 much
resembled our present-day elephant, but if anything
he was a few feet lower at the shoulder. The
general shape of his skull began to resemble our
own elephant, but the lower front teeth had now
developed into formidable tusks, which stuck out
straight in front for three or four feet, and his upper
two front teeth, instead of being curved like a
walrus's, as in Forms 1 and 2, now wents traight
out in front for over four feet, and they were
parallel to the two lower tusks. Altogether he
must have looked a very formidable creature.
The four toes, also, instead of being all separated
from one another as in Forms 1 and 2, now became
one solid foot mass, with the toe-nails situated from
the actual toe-bones, as you see in the modern
elephant.

The next stage was the appearance of the mammoth and our present-day elephant.

All these ancestors of our elephant thrived in
various countries : West and North-West America,
in India, Africa and Europe. I do not wish you
to think that these were the only localities where
they existed. It so happened that certain geological
formations were happily presented to scientists in
these regions, on the slopes of massive strata, where
wind, water and the untiring hand of time had
exposed the precious secrets of the apparently endless
past.

We have now arrived at the time when there
were elephants in the world contemporarily with
primitive man, which geologically speaking was

only about the day before yesterday, and from him we have recovered a few scattered line drawings, scratched on bits of ivory, of the great mammoth. This elephant was the largest of all known species, past or present, for it had a height at the shoulder of about fifteen feet.

It may interest you to know that these animals were numerous in England and fairly plentiful in Scotland during what is called the pre-glacial period.

These mammoths roamed in great herds over the whole of Russia and Siberia, and when the northern part of that region came under the grip of the ever-extending severe cold from the North Pole, hundreds upon hundreds of them used to accidentally get bogged, and their vast bulk sank them deep into the mire. Here they froze literally solid, and many complete specimens have been found in the north of Russia with all the hair on their skins well preserved, and in one case even the last bit of grass he had been chewing remained fixed between the great molar teeth.

The average height of this elephant, as mentioned just now, was fifteen feet, while a very big modern African elephant is only eleven feet. This mammoth was completely covered with thick, yellowy-red hair, and his tusks were as proportionately large as his body. They were curved upwards and backwards, but the reason for this I will reserve until I come to the subject of ivory in general. The cause of the extinction of the mammoth was undoubtedly the relentless advance of practically permanent Arctic conditions over the entire northern area of Russia and Siberia.

We have approached the time when all forms of

elephants had become extinct in North and North-West America and Southern Europe, also the mammoth frozen out of Northern Europe, but two distinct types were gradually being evolved in India and the vast continent of Africa, and the elephant, as we see him to-day in these two regions, was approximately the same to look at as he was at the time of the mammoth's extinction.

Most of us have seen elephants in zoos or circuses, but few, I venture to say, could have determined at a glance if the animals belonged to either the Indian or African species. Briefly the obvious external differences are as follow :

The Indian elephant differs from the African in the following main features : The forehead is extremely flat—in fact, it appears almost concave—while in the African it is distinctly rounded if looked at from the side. The ears of the Indian are ridiculously small compared with the African.

In height and bulk generally the Indian is markedly the smaller animal. The hide of the Indian is almost devoid of any hairs, while the African is covered with short, black, bristly hair three-quarters of an inch in length. The back of the Indian is distinctly more arched and curved than that of the African, and finally the forefeet have five toe-nails and the hind feet four, while the African has only three fully developed on the hind foot.

There is still one infallible guide to determine the two elephants by, and that is the tip of the trunk. The Indian elephant has one sort of finger-like projection from the upper end of the trunk, while the African has two such fingers, one on the upper and one on the lower, to facilitate the picking up of small articles of food.

In ninety out of a hundred elephants seen in zoological gardens and circuses you will find them to be of the Indian species. The reason for this is not that there are more elephants in India than in Africa, but because the African elephant so often develops recurrent phases of savageness (especially the males) and marked ill temper as soon as they become fully adult.

You can well imagine the risk to the lives of the attendants and keepers and the damage that a semi-mad, full-grown elephant could do in a short time, and it is for this reason that you will see so few African elephants in captivity.

In India it has been the practice for thousands of years to utilize the elephant as a domestic beast of burden.

Historically we all remember when at school being taught about the great military genius, Hannibal, attacking the Roman Empire. Hannibal lived some 2,200 years ago, and was a Carthaginian, which was in the north of Africa. In one of his invasions he employed about forty elephants, not for transport, but as a fighting unit, and he complained bitterly over the fact that the Roman elephants, which were imported from India, were so much stronger and more skilful than his own. Now the African elephant is larger than the Indian one, and there were never any elephants in the part of Africa called Carthaginia. Hannibal's elephants must have been Sudanese animals, and you will remember I have told you how dangerous and difficult it is to handle full-grown African elephants. Therefore Hannibal's elephants can only have been immature specimens, which accounts for their being smaller and less skilful than the highly trained adult Indian elephants possessed by the Romans.

This is very interesting as being about the earliest chronological data existing concerning the difference between the Indian and African elephants, and probably this is the first occasion on which African elephants were used for utilitarian purposes.

Since the Indian elephant will not breed to any appreciable extent in captivity, the stock of domesticated animals has to be continually replenished by the capture of wild individuals, and I now propose to briefly describe how they do catch elephants in India.

The only method of capturing an entire herd is by employing the *keddah* system. *Keddah* is, I believe, the Hindustani name for a stockade enclosure. The general procedure is as follows : An elephant-catching party, termed a *keddah* party, comprises some 400 men, who go out during the winter prepared to stay two or three months in the forests. When a herd is discovered the party divide and go off in different directions, so as to surround it, leaving two men at a distance of fifty yards or so. When completed the circle should have a circumference of from six to eight miles, and when once a herd is found and surrounded it must be the fault of the men if the herd is not captured.

The circle of men having been formed, the first thing to do is to rapidly form a light fence of split bamboos, and also rough shelters for the men. The elephants are then kept within the circle by firing shots by day and by lighting fires by night. After the first few days, however, if the ring is sufficiently large, say a full eight miles all round, and there happens to be a fair amount of good dense cover, the herd gives but little trouble.

Somewhere in the circle, as near the middle as possible, the construction of the *keddah* or stockade fence is pushed on with all possible speed. A great deal of skill and knowledge is required in order to select the best site in which to put the *keddah*, for it must be so blinded by the natural forest growth that the herd, when gradually moving towards it, may be almost completely trapped before it becomes aware of the complete enclosure.

The posts of the *keddah* are very massive, about one foot in diameter and twelve feet in height, supported by numerous outside props, and arranged in a circle of fifty yards or so in diameter. In front of this there are two diverging lines of routes flanked by big posts, extending for 100 yards, but as the route is a curved one, they both meet at the drop gate of the real trap or *keddah* enclosure.

When all this has been thoroughly prepared the herd is very cautiously driven towards the entrance-ways, and once they consent to travel along these the success of the drive is assured. They pass slowly along, packed close together, and have no option but to enter the stockade, owing to the pressure of numbers crowding up behind. As soon as the *keddah* is full, or before a stampede occurs, the drop gate over the entrance is released, and three months' arduous labour and continuous anxiety is over.

The captured elephants are subsequently man-handled by most expert and daring elephant tamers, with the aid of trained cow elephants, who most cunningly occupy the captive's entire attention, while a native slips off her back and actually ties up with a rope the hind legs of the wild elephant. I can imagine no more wonderful daring than to accomplish this feat, not once but continually, for twenty or thirty times in succession, among a herd of exasperatedly maddened wild elephants.

About fifteen years ago the British Government attempted the experiment of capturing wild elephants in Uganda, in Central Africa. They employed some trained Indian cow elephants, accustomed to the work, and eight Indian professionals. The method adopted was not the *keddah* system I have just attempted to describe, but that of the cows dancing attendance on solitary bull elephants so persistently and continuously that he got no time to rest or sleep. After a few days of this an attempt was made to tie up the hind legs, when he was allowed to snatch a little sleep. Though a few such attempts were made, the only result was the killing of six out of the eight Indian professional catchers. The remaining two were then quite prepared to swim back to Bombay rather than remain in the land of the African elephant. I also believe, although I cannot absolutely vouch for it, that the trained Indian cow elephants died very shortly after in Central Africa, from the insufficiency of the supply of curry and rice.

Turning now to the continent of Africa, which some scientists believe to have been the actual home of the primitive ancestor of our modern elephant, we know that not very long ago, historically, practically the whole of Africa supported vast herds of elephants. From a little south of Khartoum to the sea beaches of Cape Town, and from near the mouth of the Congo River to within sight of the Indian Ocean in East Africa, the elephant used to roam in vast numbers. This area is really huge, and may be estimated at about five million odd square miles. Of course, I don't mean that this entire area was uniformly stocked with elephants, but that suitable elephant country was to be found everywhere.

The African elephant never had an enemy excepting man, and in the long, long ago a very large portion of Africa was inhabited solely by a race of dwarf negroes, whose attempts at elephant destruction were presumably not very persistent. Of course, ever since the times of earliest records, the mention of ivory as a treasure invariably asserts itself, and even now, in 1921, it commands a very high value. So we must presume that the African elephant has from time immemorial been hunted primarily for food, with its ivory as a good commercial by-product.

There were various methods of hunting elephants in Africa in prehistoric times, and some of these are still practised in the identical system among modern savage tribes. At the Cape Town Museum once I was privileged to be allowed to inspect the original skilful carvings made by the dwarf peoples who then populated what is now called Cape Colony. These carvings were made on solid rock which formed the walls of the caves they lived in, and they faithfully portrayed the various incidents of the hunting of many African animals. The date ascribed to these drawings was anything from five to ten thousand years ago, but they were wonderfully executed, and in many places the original paint of vegetable and clay pigment seemed quite fresh and vivid.

At least two methods of killing elephants were

employed by these little dwarf men. One was by means of pitfalls and the other by deadfalls. It is strange to relate that even now these pitfalls are only made by the under-sized natives who lead a continuous forest existence and who are very shy of white men.[1] . . . When an elephant falls into one of these pits he lurches forward, and the two forefeet go right down to the bottom, which, being only two feet in breadth, has the effect of so jamming them together by the animal's great bulk as to make them absolutely immovable. The hind legs usually crumple up on the knees, with both wedged half-way down the pit, and there the poor beast awaits starvation, or being speared to death by the little hunters. Occasionally, but only very occasionally, I have known of an elephant falling into a pit and subsequently being rescued by its companions, who have managed to tear away a portion of the sides, and then with their trunks hoist out the captive.

The other method I mentioned as being used by the prehistoric folk was that of a deadfall. This is still widely used, even far more so than the pitfall. First of all a big native iron spearhead, twelve inches long and three broad, is lashed on with hide to a stout shaft of wood three feet long. At the upper end of this a big stone, the size of a football, is ingeniously fixed, and this has a grass rope round it which is thrown round the limb of some tree, round which it is known that elephants frequently pass. The grass rope is carried to the ground, and is anchored there by a system of forked

[1] The natives in North-Eastern Rhodesia and Nyasaland sometimes tried to trap elephants in pitfalls, as I saw a number of these pits at various times and places.—D.D.L.

sticks, which also form the trigger, or releasing device, so that on an elephant treading on it, down comes the whole contraption, and the spear is deeply embedded in the neck or forequarters of the elephant, who staggers on and dies of exhaustion.

Some tribes only use a light stone as a weight, but then they put poison on the iron point, and follow the elephant tracks for perhaps many miles till they come upon him dead.

It may seem strange that the natives eat the meat of an elephant killed by such a poisoned spear, or by numerous poisoned arrows, with impunity and immunity.

There is a method of catching elephants alive by means of a snare, which has rather restricted use. You would think that it would require a good thick wire rope about the size of your wrist to successfully anchor a very animated five-ton elephant, but the native snare is nothing more than the green bark of a tree tightly twisted. A loop is formed and passed round the main portion when this strange rope is green, and it is secured to a tree which happens to be a favourite resting-place during the heat of the day for elephants. It is supported a few inches off the ground, in the form of a huge loop, by small forked sticks, and occasionally an elephant happens to get a foot planted into one, and the natives finish him off by poisoned arrows at a safe distance.

About the most barbarous of all native methods is the one in which they employ fire. There are two Central African tribes who practise this annually, on account of the nature of the ground lending itself to the easy destruction of many elephants in one operation. The most favourable site is a large

area, say eight or ten miles of so-called elephant
grass. Why it is called so, I could never quite
make out. Elephants never eat it, and only roam
about in it if the scrub bush of the locality is too
sparse to afford shade during the hottest hours of
the day.

It is certainly an elephantine type of grass, being
eight or twelve feet in height, and as thick as your
little finger. If you are bold enough to go hunting
for elephant in this grass, you can only move in
the lanes the elephants have made, as you cannot
force your way through it for many yards without
the utmost exertion. Some of these large patches
of elephant grass have a rough semicircular ring
of steep low hills skirting about half-way round the
grass plain. During the dry season this grass
burns like so much dry paper, and if a luckless herd
of elephants happens to be frequenting such a suitable spot during the dry season, arrangements are
quickly made to encompass its destruction.

Two hundred or more natives surround the
grass area, and the grass is set alight on a given signal
on the entire side facing the steep semicircular
hills.

A constant din is kept up by yelling and the beating
of drums, while the elephants, scared by the smoke
and noise, retire towards the steep hills. The
natives wear thick ox-hide sandals for this form of
hunting, which effectually protect their feet, and as
the area of burnt grass grows smaller and smaller,
the hunters are drawn closer to each other.

Eventually the panic-stricken herd try to escape
by the steep hills, but are easily scared off by the
active niggers scrambling about yelling at them, and
they are compelled to remain stampeding till the

fire reaches and passes them. They then make a break for the open country, but their feet have now become so scorched that many find it impossible to move a yard. Poisoned arrows do the rest, and perhaps twenty or more of the herd, bulls, cows and little ones, lie dead on the ashes of the plain.

I am going to make now what must strike you as a most improbable statement, but all the same it is a positive fact, and it is that no white man and no natives I have yet been familiar with have ever seen an elephant dead from natural causes.

It is surely most remarkable that an animal the bulk of a fair-sized stack of hay should never have been seen by anyone lying dead in the African bush from old age or disease. I will readily explain the reason why a little later on, but I mention the fact now, just after I have been telling you about the natives killing elephants by the help of fire, for the following reason.

A certain rather noted African traveller, much addicted to the writing of books to relate his experiences and adventures, once wrote a long account of having at last discovered an elephant cemetery. It was a most vivid piece of impressional English, backed up by a huge picture of a huge pile of elephant skeletons, with tusks of a record size sticking out of the pile in all directions. What the author had really come across was the skeletons of a few elephants that had perished in one of these fire massacres, and whose bleached bones lay fairly close together, as they probably died standing all bunched together for mutual protection. This, I think, is a fairly good example of what is called " A Traveller's Tale."

Man, I fear, must be characterized as the most predatory and destructive of all animals, but with regard to the killing of elephants I am sure the white man carries more on his conscience than the native. The latter hunts and slays for meat and hide as well as ivory, while the white man shoots for ivory alone. The elephant has not a single enemy to fear excepting man, and he alone persistently destroys him, mainly for the sake of the unique material—ivory.

In the early part of my remarks I told you I would give you some information concerning ivory : the elephant, the walrus and the narwal. The teeth of the hippopotamus might possibly be included as a very poor form of ivory. Commercially speaking we may discount all and speak of elephant ivory as the only real article. Every animal's teeth, including our own, are composed of two substances, namely dentine in bulk, and an outer layer of very hard stuff called enamel. Elephant ivory is composed of pure dentine and nothing else. It is soft,[1] and lends itself to all sorts of artistic carving. In its natural form as a tusk it has a most beautiful texture, and is good to look upon without any artificial embellishment. You would have thought that, being such an expensive and much-sought-after article, it would have been produced synthetically and advertised as something "just as good as ivory." Many of Nature's pure products that are in great demand are commercially imitated, such as synthetic rubber,

---

[1] As a matter of fact, though ivory may be called soft, ivory merchants speak of ivory as being "soft" and "hard." It is only comparatively "hard," but the "soft" brings the best price in the market.—D.D.L.

which, I believe, is a first-class substitute, synthetic paraffin, from a low-grade brown coal, and, of course, "made in Germany"; synthetic diamonds can also be made, but they are so small, and so costly to produce, that it does not pay to make them. Ivory comes under this last category.

Some ten or twelve years ago a Russian scientist managed to produce a substance that so nearly resembled real ivory that it required an expert with a microscope to detect the difference. This synthetic ivory was made out of milk, chemically treated, and most forcibly compressed. The result was a splendid imitation, but the finished product was more expensive than the natural ivory; therefore you may say there is no substitute for real ivory.

The baby elephant is born with distinct, but, of course, very diminutive tusks, and, contrary to all other forms of teeth, these tusks never stop growing during the entire life of the elephant. The reason why they are restricted in length is because they are continually being used for digging up roots of small trees and the prodding about in hard soil impregnated with salt, for elephants, like nearly all animals, are very fond of what is called in Africa a " salt lick."

It might be noted in passing that elephants are very much inclined to be, so to speak, right-handed; that is to say they more usually employ the right tusk to do the grubbing work with. Occasionally one finds an elephant who either does very little prodding with either of his tusks, or else his tusks have a tendency to abnormally quick growth, with the result that both his tusks almost reach to the ground.

In the case of the present elephant's immediate ancestor, the mammoth, his tusks assumed a decided upward curved tendency from a very early age, and in consequence these grew on and on, in a huge curve, often reaching the total length of twelve feet. The record weight of a pair of elephant's tusks is now 228 or 230 lbs. each—that is, over 450 lbs. the pair, or a little less than four hundredweight.

This elephant was actually shot by a very much underclothed nigger, with a Tower of London musket, that he had stolen from the Germans in German East Africa.

One of these tusks is now in the British Museum, London, and its fellow was purchased by America.[1]

Ivory, like every other commodity, varies in quality, but with a little experience you can, on examining a tusk, or even a small portion of ivory, tell what part of Africa it came from. This is not so with the Indian ivory, which is very much smaller in size and more uniform in character. The present flat rate of ivory is, roughly speaking, about £1 sterling a pound.[2]

Many years ago I saw a sight in the Congo I shall never forget, and that was a big chief's grass hut in which all the supports were composed of

[1] The tusk which is a supposed pair to the one in the Natural History Museum did not go to America, but on the date I write (2/4/33) belongs, as I previously mention, to Mr. V. Myers, of the firm of M. Myers, 15/20, Tower Hill, London, E.C.3. I do not believe the well-known Zanzibar photograph depicts a true pair from one elephant, as they differ so much in curve and girth. These tusks must have come from two animals.—D.D.L.

[2] As I write this, in April, 1933, the flat rate of ivory is roughly half the figure given above, as, like almost everything else, ivory has depreciated greatly.—D.D.L.

a tusk of ivory for each post, and he had a short length of fencing round his front door made of elephant tusks, placed together touching each other. I am quite sure the Belgian local authorities must have, sooner or later, discovered this extremely beautiful and valuable hutment, and speedily put a Government architect on the job in order to bring it up to Congo County Council regulations !

Elephants roam about in herds of about twenty or thirty up to some three hundred strong, and if one gets badly mixed up among the latter when trying to find the biggest tusker, the fun of the business seems suddenly to disappear, but, after all, the true Britisher never enjoys a sporting venture so much as when the odds are most heavily against him. These herds lead a most peaceful life, as a general rule, and they have periodical migrations from place to place, according to the wet and dry seasons of the year.

Young elephants, soon after birth, are most nimble and very frisky little fellows of some two and a half feet high. They can travel with the herd quite easily, as the pace is seldom more than a mile an hour normally. If a youngster gets into difficulties in a dry river-bed, or some hollow in the ground with undergrowth in it, and is missed by its mother, it begins to call for help. The mother returns at her best pace, about ten miles an hour, with her huge ears spread out at right angles to her head, until she stands over the struggling calf, and there she stands and stares at it for a few moments. Suddenly her mind is made up, and she hoists the infant out with her trunk, puts it on the trail she has taken to come back to it, and then soundly spanks it for getting into difficulties.

Even with full-grown elephants, if one of the herd, especially if it be a cow, gets into trouble of any sort, two or more of the herd will at once come to its assistance, and not leave it till matters are all right again.[1]

The young elephant grows very slowly, and does not arrive at maturity till about thirty years old. It passes a most peaceful existence but for the occasional scares and encounters with man, its only object of fear, and its life is passed in a most leisurely manner, roaming and browsing, and migrating according to the seasons.

Some authorities hold that an elephant never lies down, and that if it is compelled to do so by illness or accident, it cannot rise again. This, I think, is quite untrue. I have often seen places where they have lain down [So have I.—D.D.L.], but these places have always been selected on the side of a fairly steep bank [Often on the side of a big anthill, too.—D.D.L.], whereby the process of getting on to their feet again has been rendered comparatively easy. Normally elephants rest and sleep standing up, but they often select a good big tree to lean against, and if they start to rub that tree after a sleep, the result is a bit of polished wood like an old mahogany table.

As time goes on, and they begin to get old, the bulls go off, and either lead a solitary existence, or else half a dozen club together and form a herd of their own. The old cows wander about, and

1 Some people deny that elephants help one another, but Cuninghame, who had great experience, has evidently seen the actions he mentions. Personally I have twice seen elephants aid one another, so I know it does occur occasionally. Certainly it must happen oftenest in the case of a cow elephant and her calf when the maternal instinct is displayed.—D.D.L.

journey with any herd they happen to affiliate themselves with.

Senility, or old age, is now becoming apparent, but the question arises : What is the age of an old elephant, either African or Indian? In neither continent has a definite decision been reached as to the normal longevity of an elephant. In India, owing to the practice of capture by the *keddah* method, it has been possible to have elephants in captivity under records of well over 100 years, but it has not been determined with any certainty how old the captives were when captured. . . . He may perhaps live, say, 100 to 125 years, which, I expect, is a good deal older than any of us want to live to.

When an elephant, he or she, reaches a really advanced stage of life, or if through illness, or some disease, the elephant feels the premonition of impending death, they, like every other animal, seek the depths of solitude. The old or sick elephant detaches itself from its companions, and moves away alone. It endeavours to find the very densest patch of forest it has strength to penetrate. Having forced its way in, it stands till it drops of exhaustion and dies unknown or unseen by man or beast. Soon the leopards, hyenas, jackals, foxes, rats and mice, and the rest of the forest scavengers appear, and little is soon to be found of the mighty elephant. In an incredibly short time the displaced tropical forest growth has completely covered what the hungry carrion feeders have left, and this is the explanation of why no white man or native has ever found a naturally dead elephant.[1]

See footnote opposite page

Notes for a Lecture in New Galloway

By R. J. Cuninghame, M.C.

Most of you are here this evening with the anticipation that you are to listen to travel talk, but in reality what I am going to talk about are traveller's tales connected with a hunter's life in Central Africa, and to give you some idea of its many incidents.

A hunter's life is full of peculiar experiences, but I regret I cannot afford you a detailed description of hairbreadth escapes from death while I was engaged in the pursuit of the world's largest and most dangerous animals, as fortunately they did not often occur.

The lack of sensational experiences was due to the fact that throughout the long period of some twenty-three years, during which I followed the adventurous life of a professional big-game and elephant hunter, the combination of fate, good luck, and some degree of being able to shoot accurately with the heaviest kind of both ancient and modern rifles was always on my side. This happy combination enabled me to escape serious trouble, and it also helped to preserve the lives of those who entrusted themselves to my care when they wanted to go in for a serious big-game hunting expedition in Africa.

---

[1] Doubtless some elephants die in thick bush or forest, but their remains in this case would some day be found occasionally. Personally I am sure the reason so few skeletons are found is because dying elephants get bogged in soft, wet ground, and disappear completely. There was an extremely interesting photograph of this actually happening published in *East Africa* on April 10th, 1930.—D.D.L.

Now in talking of risks in hunting dangerous animals it is interesting to compare the proportion of risk run by the old-timers, such as Gordon-Cumming, Samuel Baker, Selous and a few others. These men were armed with muzzle-loading rifles and usually they were only single barrelled.

In South Africa, that is, south of the Zambezi river, where these men were hunting, they hunted mostly on horseback. This was about the time of 1840 to 1870. They had to carry their powder, and keep it dry in the tropical rains, carry their spherical soft lead bullets in one bag, and the wadding in another. They used enormous charges of coarse black powder, which produced a low-lying dense belt of thick grey smoke, which, under adverse conditions, completely obscured the lion or buffalo they had fired at. After firing they had to clamber on to a horse with some 15 to 18 lbs. weight of blunderbuss in one hand, gallop off over any sort of rough ground, and while so doing start laboriously to reload with a long ramrod while going full speed.

The pluck, skill and physical strength required of these hunters far surpasses, in my opinion, that required of their grandsons to-day.

Most of you have some acquaintance of a modern rifle, and a big-game rifle is only a magnified example of that type. With it you can carry two or three dozen cartridges in a bandolier, and it does not matter how wet they get, while the accuracy of direction and the penetration on impact is vastly superior in efficiency to the clumsy weapons of olden days.

In addition to this the habits of African big game in the old hunter's days had not been disturbed by the white man's civilization to any extent. There were no railways, telegraphs and steamers to and fro on the various waterways, necessitating the continual presence of numerous white men and their required habitations.

The big game of Africa had seldom heard the explosion of gunpowder, and consequently regarded the white hunter as on the same footing as the native with his spear and bow and arrow. The elephants, buffaloes and lions roamed about by day in the self-conscious superiority that they were the actual lords and masters of the particular area they lived in. This fact, coupled with the greater abundance of dangerous game inhabiting a good game locality, greatly increased the danger incurred to those intrepid pioneers who taught us how to tackle successfully the fiercest of animals with about the most elementary form of fire-arms.[1]

The last time I had the pleasure of addressing you here my subject was "The Life History of the Elephant," from the time it started its evolution as a little animal, no bigger than a good-sized fat pig, to the five-ton pachyderm that roams the forests to-day. I treated the subject somewhat academically, but this evening I intend to endeavour to be more discursive on personal incidents connected with elephants, lions, buffaloes, and such-like really dangerous animals.

Elephants have always been my special friends, and my very worst enemies.

[1] I can hardly agree with Cuninghame that big-game shooting to-day is less dangerous except we have the great advantage of modern rifles. Animals after much persecution get far more dangerous to tackle ; and to-day elephants, for instance, are much more liable to charge than they were long ago. This also applies to lions and buffaloes.—D.D.L.

Really to know, not all, but as much as may be possible about an individual species of wild animal you must live under the same conditions as it does, and I have with elephants done so for months at a time, the longest period extending over two consecutive years. You thus learn all the idiosyncrasies and family life history and what I may call the "herdal" proclivities. By that I mean the normal progressive routine of an elephant's existence. You discover the seasonal periods of day when it prefers to feed, rest, sleep and travel. What it will feed on in certain localities, and when it requires salt, on account of eating continuously certain foods and a host of other natural details of its general routine of life.

While you are engaged in all these things you must perfect yourself by hard experience and anatomical study as to how and where to manœuvre and shoot, so as to save yourself from fatal consequences in the event of your having effectually disposed of one elephant and finding you are up against two or three more who are bent on giving trouble at close quarters in either comparatively open country, thick bush, or dense forest or grass.

It is quite an interesting and exciting sporting study, and it applies equally to the handling of any of Africa's really dangerous big game.

Many has been the true hunter who has lost his life, not from foolhardiness or bad marksmanship, but simply from the fact that certain members of the animal kingdom are possessed of a vitality after receiving a mortal wound far exceeding that of human beings.

I am supposed to give you some stories this

evening—some distant relative of George Washington!

I will now give you an instance of an elephant's
vitality. A certain Government official in the
Uganda Colony of Central Africa, many years
ago, was stationed in a really good elephant country,
and one day he thought he would try to get an
elephant. He had never even seen one and knew
nothing of the " game."

As a precautionary measure he took out with
him six native soldiers armed with Martini-Henry
rifles, and had himself (this was in the year 1902)
a modern high-velocity small-bore rifle. There
were fired in all fifty-two shots. This will show
you the necessity of having an accurate knowledge
of how to shoot a single bull elephant, let alone
having to manœuvre and escape the attentions of
a whole herd, who will be mostly cows, and much
more aggressive than herd bulls.

Before you attempt to tackle any species of
dangerous big game (African, or of any other
country) you should carefully study anatomically
the two or three vital areas, and the angles from
which you can place a fatal shot therein.

(Now discuss on where and how you can shoot
an elephant. Brain, heart, lumbar, and tell stories.)

(1) I have fortunately never had a fatal accident
when hunting elephant, but I very nearly had when
out with a man who was learning how to shoot
elephants.

Allan Black and I were both charged at the
same time by two elephants. I got mine. Black
was knocked unconscious. Arm and ribs broken.

(2) How Powell was not so lucky. He had no
experience. Failed to stop his elephant in open

country. He ran, was caught, and had his legs and arms plucked off!

(3) Self in Congo with a pigmy, and 300 elephants all round. Pigmy made a noise like a frog and we got through!

(4) Roosevelt's first elephant. How he got the one he was after in densest bush, and then two others charged us. I got mine and I thought T.R. would have been killed by the other.

(5) How Roosevelt blew me off the fallen tree!

(6) Photographing cows with S. Nöegren, when I killed leading cow, having only two cartridges.

(7) My Wanderobo mystic rights to bring good sport.

(8) Mrs. Akeley's good elephant.

(9) I have now something to tell you "in strict confidence." At one period of my career I was an elephant poacher. Six of us started for the Congo from East Africa and got there in two months, and started operations.

In six months only two of us were left. Two died of fever, one was killed by an elephant and one was killed by Congo cannibals.

A man named Darley and myself were left!

We agreed to each share a big bit of Africa, each taking about 105,000 square miles, i.e., about 400 N. and S., and 300 E. and W.

The respective authorities of the Congo, Uganda, and the Sudan never seriously tried to catch us, but I must say occasionally they made us march for a month or two in order to escape into another part of Africa. We were eventually called the two "Robbers of the North," meaning that we operated north of the Equator.

There is now thirty tons of ivory buried in gravel, value to-day in the market about £60,000.

For two years I was what may be called a fugitive from justice, then I became a reformed character !

Darley would not and continued for one year longer. We only met twice in two years, the country being so huge, and every native was our friend and private detective for the sake of so much meat.

The best day's work I did was bagging six good elephants before breakfast one morning.

(10) On returning to civilization I was put on to the International Committee to suggest new laws, in order to preserve elephants ! That sounds rather strange, does it not ?

When Darley ceased to poach elephants the Colonial thought so much of him, etc. Give an account of the Abyssinian trip with scorpion story and ending with his C.M.G. !

(11) Mention that when in the Southern Sudan I tried hunting with the Hamran Arabs, etc.

Swords from Solingen (Germany) !

How they hamstring an elephant, or cut off the trunk when charged.

Now I think I must leave elephant stories and give a few lion recollections.

In hunting lions you have a vastly different proposition to that of the pursuit of elephants.

Elephants in the old-time days behaved exactly as they do now,[1] but lions, generally speaking, all

---

[1] I cannot agree to this as much hunting and wounding have made elephants more aggressive as time goes on than they formerly were ; but, of course, this is simply a matter of individual opinion. —D.D.L.

over Africa have modified their habits in conformity with the advance of civilization.

In the days when the Roman Empire was at its zenith lions were very plentiful throughout Asia, Mesopotamia and Northern Somaliland. [Also in Algeria.—D.D.L.]

It is recorded that 600 captured live lions were delivered in one year at Rome to provide " sport " for the population when they went to the arenas to witness either the unequal contests between slaves trained as gladiators, or the killing of early Christians, by the method of herding them in the arenas, and then releasing semi-starved lions and lionesses to kill and gorge themselves on the helpless victims.

A hundred years ago, when the pioneer hunters used the muzzle-loading blackpowder guns, lions in Africa were by no means scared by the sight of a white man, and they regarded and respected him no more than they did the indigenous nigger of the country. Their habits were far more diurnal than nocturnal, and they went abroad up till about eight or nine in the morning, leaving their lairs again at four or five in the afternoon.

They were much more audacious when tackled in the open in daytime, and, generally speaking, they conformed in a higher degree than they do to-day to the proud position of being " The King of Beasts." During the last thirty years lions everywhere seem to have developed the sense of rapidly appreciating danger whenever a human being appears in view, especially a white man.

A lion is rarely found these days out of bed before six o'clock in the evening (which is just about continual sunset-time near the Equator), and he has returned home at sunrise whether he is hungry or not.

Although the lion's habit of life has changed along with the circumstances, his true nature has remained the same as ever.

If surprised or disturbed by man, his first instinct is to clear off and create no trouble—and that is exactly the same instinct that pervades all animals and birds that have had any experience with man.

In the remote Antarctic ice, where man is hardly ever seen, the seals and penguins there have absolutely no fear of man at all.

But to return to lions. Once you round up a lion, and he finds that the odds are against him, there is no living animal that will display more desperate fighting courage, even when mortally wounded and apparently just about to expire, than the mighty lion.

When next you happen to see the Royal Standard flying I hope you will remember this really accurate description of the main supporter of our Empire's national emblem. . . .

However, as I remarked over elephants, you must study closely the anatomy of the vital points. Here you will find the problem of how best to put a bullet into a tiny space, and into an animal rushing at high speed, through bushes, grass and stuff that practically conceals the entire beast.

Stories :

(1) Talk about the brain shot when charging and hitting an eye, and how you can do no real damage. Give Percival's example.

(2) Then the heart shot, and how I was stalking a sable antelope, and found I was being stalked by

a lion, with the result that he charged and killed my native, though the heart was hit to a pulp.

(3) How, though I said lions never took the first offensive, a lion charged out of a donga as I was passing him and I shot him with rifle fired from the hip.

(4) How I have had a few mauling accidents, and how gruesome, painful and disastrous they usually are.

Describe Dutchman's mauling when he was down with a lion mauling him. How I tried to hit the spine, but hit the hips at close range. How it failed, but gave me a chance at the neck, and how I took the putrid man to hospital. How he lived, but was a cripple for life.

(5) Galloping lions. How you have to train horses to it. The good riding and strength required with a heavy rifle. The nerve and skill required when it comes to a fight to a finish with all the grunts and roars. How a lion goes a hundred yards in six seconds, or about sixteen or seventeen yards a second, and at great bounding leaps. How a lion never starts to charge unless he means not to stop trying to kill you, or unless you kill him first.

There is no low cunning about a lion. When he starts business his mane rises straight up on end, his tail gives premonitory recurrent twitches, and when he starts coming with a roar and continuous horrible grunts nothing but death can stop him.

Now tell stories.

(6) How little T. [Tarleton ?] shot a charging lion with his native gun-bearer crouching beside him saying "Thank you, master" every time the lion was hit!

(7) How Roosevelt wounded a lion, and could

not see it from a little hill even with glasses. I stirred it up, and then he got it.

(8) How the Masai can surround a lion and spear it. Two men do it and the rest close in. One or more men are generally killed over the game.

(9) Talking of Masai reminds me of how I caught a lion, which had killed some of their cattle, with flypaper. You can get it from McClintock.

(10) I never engaged much in the capture of live animals for zoos, as this can never pay well, except perhaps with Germany.

(11) Story of how I helped the German wild-animal catcher to transport his menagerie from Entebbe to the German ship at the coast.

The German went ill with fever. The giraffe could not be taken through the only tunnel, the train got on fire, the fate of the escaped. Ardvark at Mombasa up the drainpipe. Also how the lion scratched the German stoker !

I trust that some of the incidents recorded will not be treated as simply " Traveller's Tales." I can assure you that they are Tales of a Traveller, but not " Traveller's Tales."

R.J.C.

Before bringing this volume to an end there are a few subjects connected with African big game that I would like to make some remarks on.

With regard to the recent literature on the fauna and its natural history, quite a lot of cribbing from the works of former hunters takes place and these views are given as original, and no acknowledgment is made. This is, of course, unfair to the men, many of whom are dead, whose observations are filched.

Again, a dreadful amount of exaggeration occurs, and it is possible for a hunter shooting alone, without witnesses being present to authenticate his statements, to lay it on as thick as he cares to do, and he often does so, but the really experienced hunter who reads of his marvellous adventures can usually perceive his " magnifications," and pick out the deceptions from his thrilling escapes from a gory death.

But by far the worst point in fallacious information is in the matter of game measurements, for here we are dealing with supposed facts, and not personal fiction, which latter can affect nobody but the Ananias in question. When a man starts writing about gigantic elephants, lions or tigers he should certainly supply sound and veracious testimony as to the facts of the case if he expects naturalists to believe him. It is true that he may be hunting alone, and find it difficult to find witnesses to corroborate his word, but this is exceptional if there are white men within, say, fifty miles of him. If I had the luck to shoot a twelve-foot lion, I would at once send runners off with messages to several of my friends to come at once to the scene, and I would certainly keep every bone of such a remarkable specimen for future examination by experts.

Some years ago two viceroys in India, whose names it is unnecessary to mention, had, during their terms of office, the gratification of each shooting a " record " tiger, which was, I presume, measured by their aide-de-camp or by their native shikaris.

Mr. A. A. Dunbar-Brander, whose name is so well known in connection with Indian sport and

DENIS D. LYELL

natural history, has dealt with the matter of these specimens of " Felis tigris superbus " in the columns of the *Field*, so not being an authority on Indian game, I need not discuss the matter here. The incidents, however, inspired me to write the following atrocious doggerel verses on the noteworthy viceregal tigers, and here they are :

IN GANDHI-LAND

In Gandhi-land the tigers grow
The most colossal skins, you know,
And felines there aspire to fame
In R. Ward's " Records of Big Game."

Some think they only swell with joy
When scenting a new viceroy,
Others perchance might blame the tape,
While most can simply gasp and gape.

The panther, snake and crocodile
Will soon awaken, stretch and smile ;
One can't expect a vile disease
To stop at tigers, if you please.

Perhaps those tapes that " take the bun "
Have got a nasty " touch of sun ";
Perhaps they will not " pull my leg "
When measuring from " peg to peg."

In the *Field* of August 5th, 1933, there appeared a letter signed Arme Blanche entitled " Special Tapes for Measuring Tigers," in which is the statement that native chiefs in India supply shikaris with special tapes on which one-inch is marked about 9/10ths only, and the Editor in a footnote adds : " This is a well-known trick. Special tapes have been known to be used by Cashmere shikaris."

So much for statistics referring to Indian tigers. I never heard of special tapes of this kind being used in South Central Africa, and if a man wants to exaggerate the dimensions of a beast, or its head, when it grows horns, it is easy with an ordinary tape to add many fictitious inches to a measurement, by working the tape along curves in the body, or pressing it into hollows along a horn. The correct way to measure a beast is to stretch it out flat and put a peg in the ground at its snout and another where the skin ends on the tail, seeing that these pegs or sticks are absolutely standing vertical. With long sticks fixed against an elephant's shoulder and flat of a forefoot it is easy to make a measurement quite six inches more by bending each stick in an outward direction.

To-day men and women are taking more interest in game photography than in hunting and killing, and this is a good thing in so far as it will tend to the survival of the fauna in the future. The former, however, notwithstanding the statements of the photographers, lacks grave risks, and although it may seem to be as perilous to approach dangerous game with a camera as with a rifle the risks are very much less, as dangerous game very seldom act on the offensive until they are made furious by a painful wound. This is absolutely true, for the first instinct of all wild animals is to bolt as soon as they scent, hear or see a human being.

In photography a tele-photo lens does good work at some distance, and the only danger in going in close with a camera is the slight possibility of approaching a female with young, or a beast previously wounded, which, of course, may take reprisals with dire results.

Some of the titles on latter-day big-game books are rather melodramatic, and might do for the advertisement on a hoarding of some film pictures, and when this is so the contents usually are in keeping with the title. I cannot imagine men like Selous, Neumann, Stigand or Bell naming a volume in such a sensational way, but it is a period of superlatives in more senses than one. There have been few books written on big game recently which can ever become standard works, and which one would care to add to one's library, or read more than once.

Writing books on big game and natural history seldom pays the author, and the craze for photography does not pay the rifle-maker or taxidermist, for to-day the sale of rifles and the work of setting up specimens must have depreciated greatly and caused financial loss to many expert workmen in both these trades.

It is my opinion that the men who lived for the fifty years preceding the Great War of 1914–18 saw the best of things in the way of wild sport. In their lifetime rifles improved marvellously, and communications became better, enabling them to get to game countries where special forms of game could be procured. For instance, that fine shot Littledale went to the Pamir and got splendid specimens of ovispoli and other mountain game, Radclyffe, Millais and others shot great-horned moose in the Kenai, and Selous did the same in the Yukon, and he broke fresh ground after caribou in Newfoundland. It was an expensive business, but nothing like what it became after the Great War.

The travel expenses were not the sole outlay, for it cost a large sum to get the trophies mounted, and to-day, with fewer men going in for wild sport, the taxidermists—some of whom are artistic experts—must be feeling the pinch. The same applies to another body of splendid workmen—the rifle-makers, as for three good weapons they sold long ago I do not suppose they dispose of one to-day.

The value of well-mounted game specimens is little in pounds, shillings and pence, for I have seen a noted big-game hunter's collection go for a few shillings, and even pence a head, and when I remembered how he valued them I could not help thinking how futile are a man's strivings to obtain (often with considerable patience and hardship) something that nobody appreciates but himself.

If the big game of the world is to be preserved, it is essential that our Colonial Governments should take more interest in the matter than is being done to-day, and they can do little without the authority of our home Government. Naturally the protection of the game costs money, as the nefarious killing of animals can only be stopped by appointing wardens and rangers to supervise the reserves. With regard to the areas which can be shot by licence-holders, the officials should be given greater powers to stop poaching. It is my opinion that fines are little good and much more stringent methods should be enforced. For a man who slaughters game from a motor car I think the machine and his rifle should be confiscated, and regarding native poachers, who kill, in season and out, game of either sex, their weapons (usually guns of the gas-pipe variety) should certainly be taken away.

In Britain this is done with members of the poaching fraternity, and nothing but drastic action will ever stop the slaughter of game in wild countries.

The splendid fauna of the Empire is a valuable asset, so while there is time to do so the authorities should take action. Some day it may be too late, and nature-lovers of the future will be justified in looking with contempt on our present rulers, who had the power to save it from extirpation, but refrained to do so because they were too inert to realize their responsibility in the matter.

INDEX